STRESS LESS, PRAY MORE: A MINDFULNESS GUIDE FOR CHRISTIAN BUSINESSWOMEN

LOVE CHRISTOPHERS

CONTENTS

INTRODUCTION

In the whirlwind of modern business, stress often feels like an unwelcome passenger, constantly vying for the driver's seat. Christian businesswomen frequently struggle to balance professional demands, personal responsibilities, and their faith, resulting in a daunting task. However, God's infinite wisdom does not lead us to a life of constant chaos and exhaustion. He invites us to a life overflowing with peace, joy, and purpose. In this life, worry is traded for prayer, frantic schedules give way to calm intentionality, and self-reliance finds its anchor in His unwavering strength.

Stress Less, Pray More: A Mindfulness Guide for Christian Businesswomen isn't just another self-help book. It serves as a compass through the complexities of life, providing a practical, faith-centered path to help you navigate the pressures you encounter with grace and resilience. The book focuses on transforming your relationship with stress, anchoring your heart in God's presence, and allowing His promises to guide you.

Unique Features of This Book

Pursuing success can feel like an ongoing struggle for many Christian women in leadership or entrepreneurial roles, often conflicting with the peace that Scripture promises. The relentless pressure to achieve, meet deadlines, and support others can easily overshadow self-care and spiritual nourishment. This book is your lifeline.

- **Inspire Peace:** Discover how to cultivate God's peace amid the most demanding schedules.

- **Encourage Prayer:** Develop a consistent prayer practice that integrates seamlessly into your daily routine.

- **Empower Confidence:** Gain clarity, focus, and unwavering trust in God's plan to enhance your confidence in your career and personal life.

Practical Application of Mindfulness for Christian Businesswomen

Mindfulness, often associated with secular practices, becomes profoundly transformative when embraced within the context of the Christian faith. It involves being intensely aware of God's constant presence and seeking His guidance every moment. For the Christian businesswoman, mindfulness can manifest in:

- **Pausing to Pray means** turning to God throughout your day—in the quiet and chaotic moments—for guidance, strength, and unwavering gratitude.

- **Surrendering Control** means acknowledging that God is sovereign over your work and learning to release the grip of worry and anxiety.

- **Being Present means** Engaging fully with the people and tasks around you, knowing that your identity is firmly grounded in Christ, not your achievements.

Guide Overview: Content and Benefits

This guide seamlessly blends timeless biblical truths with practical, actionable strategies for cultivating mindfulness, reducing stress, and deepening one's walk with God.

- **Scriptural Insights:** Gaining wisdom and inspiration from God's Word.
- **Real-Life Examples:** Stories and anecdotes that resonate with the challenges you face.
- **Engaging Exercises:** Practical activities to help you integrate prayer and mindfulness into your daily life.

Key themes explored within these pages include:

- **Finding Rest in God** involves understanding the importance of rest for your soul and how it fuels your productivity and spiritual growth.
- **Transforming Worry into Worship:** Learning to channel stress into praise and trust, finding strength in prayer and surrender.
- **Creating Sacred Space:** Establishing moments of quiet reflection and connection with God, even on the busiest days.
- **Prioritizing What Truly Matters:** Balancing career ambitions with spiritual growth and nurturing meaningful relationships.
- **Mindful Decision-Making:** Seeking God's wisdom and guidance as you navigate essential professional and personal choices.

The Heart of the Journey

Stress Less, Pray More is more than just a stress management tool; it's an invitation to deepen your relationship with God and align your work with His divine purposes. By embracing a faith-based approach to mindfulness, you will:

- **Rediscover Joy:** Experience the overflowing joy from abiding in Christ, even during the most challenging seasons.

- **Strengthen Relationships:** Lead with grace, presence, and compassion, fostering deeper connections with colleagues, clients, and loved ones.

- **Reflect God's Light:** In your leadership, become a beacon of peace and faithfulness, inspiring others to seek God's presence.

An emphasis on finding rest in God and embracing renewal is at the core of this book's message.

In Matthew 11:28, Jesus invites, "Come to me, all you who are weary and burdened, and I will give you rest." This encapsulates the essence of Stress Less, Pray More: exchanging anxiety for unwavering trust, exhaustion for rejuvenating renewal, and self-reliance for God's enduring strength.

As you embark on this journey, may you discover the practical tools and profound insights within these pages to navigate your business and personal life with clarity, confidence, and a heart filled with God's peace. Let's begin this transformative journey together.

CHAPTER 1

UNDERSTANDING STRESS IN THE MODERN WORLD

Stress has become a pervasive presence in modern life's fast-paced pace, affecting every aspect of our being. For women balancing the intricate terrains of business, family, and personal aspirations, stress often feels like an unavoidable reality—a persistent hum in the background that threatens to overwhelm. The weight of responsibilities, the pressure to meet expectations, and the pursuit of excellence in every role can leave us feeling depleted and stretched beyond our limits.

However, as daughters of the Most High, we are not called to lives of ceaseless striving and burden. God, in His infinite wisdom, invites us to a life anchored in His peace and purpose. Scripture reassures us of this truth in 1 Peter 5:7, which urges us to *"Cast all your anxiety on Him because He cares for you"* (NIV). This divine invitation is a call to surrender our worries to the One who is infinitely capable of carrying them, enabling us to navigate the demands of life with grace and strength.

This chapter is structured to explore the physical, emotional, and mental impacts of stress, with a specific emphasis on addressing the unique challenges women face in the business world, including the juggling act, societal expectations, and gender bias in the workplace. More importantly, it offers insights into how we can approach these challenges with resilience, wisdom, and unwavering faith in God's promises.

Exploring the Various Dimensions of Stress

Stress is more than a fleeting feeling of being overwhelmed—it is a pervasive force that influences every aspect of our lives, including our physical health, emotions, and mental clarity. Recognizing stress is crucial for Christian women seeking to honor God in all aspects of their lives. When stress is acknowledged and addressed with biblical truths and practical wisdom, it becomes an opportunity to grow closer to God and embrace His peace.

Jesus' invitation in Matthew 11:28-30 (NIV) offers hope and assurance: *"Come to me, all you who are weary and burdened, and I will give you rest. Take my yoke upon you and learn from me, for I am gentle and humble in heart, and you will find rest for your souls. For my yoke is easy, and my burden is light."*

This section explores the physical manifestations of stress, how it affects our bodies, and how we can begin to address its toll through faith, self-care, and reliance on God's promises.

Physical Manifestations of Stress and Their Effects

Our bodies are equipped to manage short-term stress through the "fight or flight" response, releasing hormones such as cortisol and adrenaline to tackle sudden obstacles. However, chronic stress overstimulates this system, leading to detrimental health effects over time (Sapolsky, 2004). Below, we examine some of the most common physical symptoms of stress and their impact.

- **Sleep Disturbances:** stress is a major disruptor of sleep. Racing thoughts and unresolved worries can lead to insomnia, frequent awakenings, and poor sleep quality. Sleep deprivation compounds stress, creating a vicious cycle of exhaustion and reduced cognitive function (National Sleep Foundation, 2020).

In Psalm 127:2 (NIV), God emphasizes the importance of rest: *"In vain you rise early and stay up late, toiling for food to eat—for He grants sleep to those He loves."* Sleep is not just a physical necessity but a divine gift that restores our strength and calms our spirit.

- **Weakened immune system**: Chronic stress suppresses immune function, making the body more susceptible to infections and illnesses. Studies have shown that individuals under prolonged stress are more likely to develop colds, flu, and other ailments (Cohen, Janicki-Deverts, & Miller, 2007).

Even in times of physical vulnerability, we can find strength in God's promise from Isaiah 40:29 (NIV): *"He gives strength to the weary and increases the power of the weak."*

- **Muscle tension and pain**: Stress often manifests physically as muscle tension, particularly in the neck, shoulders, and jaw. Over time, this can lead to chronic pain, migraines, and physical discomfort (American Psychological Association, 2022).

As we carry physical burdens, we are reminded of Jesus' words in Matthew 11:30 (NIV): *"For my yoke is easy and my burden is light."* Surrendering stress to Him brings relief both physically and spiritually.

- **Digestive issues**: Stress significantly impacts the gastrointestinal system, exacerbating conditions like irritable bowel syndrome (IBS) and leading to symptoms such as nausea, diarrhea, or constipation (Mayer, 2011). The gut-brain connection highlights how stress directly affects digestion, reminding us to nurture our physical and emotional health.

David's words in Psalm 94:19 (NIV) offer comfort: *"When anxiety was great within me, your consolation brought me joy."* Leaning on God can help us find relief from the emotional and physical discomfort that stress often causes.

- **Heart health risks**: Prolonged stress increases heart rate and blood pressure, straining the cardiovascular system. Over time, this can elevate the risk of serious health issues like heart disease and stroke (American Heart Association, 2019).

Proverbs 4:23 (NIV) emphasizes the importance of guarding our hearts: *"Above all else, guard your heart, for everything you do flows from it."* Protecting our physical and spiritual hearts requires us to seek peace and trust in God's care.

Effective Strategies for Managing Physical Stress

Recognizing the physical toll of stress is the first step toward managing it. Here are practical, faith-centered strategies to help you nurture your body while trusting in God's sovereignty:

1. **Prioritize Rest and Sleep**:
   Establish a bedtime routine that includes prayer and gratitude. Reflect on Psalm 4:8 (NIV): *"In peace I will lie down and sleep, for you alone, Lord, make me dwell in safety."*

2. **Engage in Physical Activity**:
   Exercise is not just a stress reliever—it is an act of stewardship for the body God has given you. Activities like walking

in nature or gentle yoga can be paired with meditating on Scriptures like 1 Corinthians 10:31 (NIV): *"So whether you eat or drink or whatever you do, do it all for the glory of God."*

3. **Eat a Nourishing Diet**:
   Stress can disrupt healthy eating habits, but prioritizing nutrient-dense foods supports both physical and emotional well-being. Remember that nourishing your body honors God's temple (1 Corinthians 6:19-20).

4. **Practice Relaxation Techniques**:
   Incorporate moments of stillness into your day through deep breathing or progressive muscle relaxation. Use this time to meditate on verses like Isaiah 26:3 (NIV): *"You will keep in perfect peace those whose minds are steadfast, because they trust in you."*

5. **Seek Medical and Professional Help When Needed**:
   There is no shame in seeking professional support for managing chronic stress. God works through medical experts and counselors to bring healing and wisdom (Proverbs 15:22).

Reflecting on God's Provision

The physical effects of stress remind us of our human limitations and the need for God's sustaining power. He created us to rely on Him, and His promises provide strength and peace even in the most challenging seasons.

As you navigate the physical manifestations of stress, remember Philippians 4:13 (NIV): *"I can do all this through Him who gives me strength."* This truth equips us to face each day with confidence, knowing that God's strength is sufficient for every burden we carry.

The Emotional Impact of Stress

The emotional effects of stress can be just as debilitating as its physical manifestations. Stress often creates a cycle of worry and fear, which affects relationships and overall happiness. According to the American Psychological Association (2022), stress commonly triggers:

- **Anxiety and worry**: A constant state of unease that feels inescapable.
- **Irritability and frustration**: Short tempers that strain relationships at home and work.
- **Feelings of overwhelm and helplessness**: The sense of drowning under responsibilities.
- **Depression and hopelessness**: A prolonged state of sadness and despair.

The Bible provides comfort for those struggling emotionally, reminding us in Psalm 34:18 that *"The Lord is close to the brokenhearted and saves those who are crushed in spirit."* This assurance encourages us to lean on God for emotional healing.

The Mental Strain of Stress

Stress is not only a physical and emotional challenge—it deeply impacts our cognitive abilities, shaping how we think, process information, and make decisions. Chronic stress, in particular, disrupts the brain's natural functioning, affecting memory, focus, and judgment. Prolonged stress can cause the mind to feel chaotic, making even the simplest tasks difficult to navigate.

Scientific studies confirm that stress has significant effects on cognitive function. According to Sandi (2013), stress alters brain activity in areas responsible for memory, concentration, and decision-making.

While these impacts are challenging, they also serve as a reminder of our need to lean on God's wisdom rather than our own understanding.

Proverbs 3:5-6 (NIV) offers this timeless truth: *"Trust in the Lord with all your heart and lean not on your own understanding; in all your ways submit to him, and he will make your paths straight."* When stress clouds our minds, this verse reassures us that seeking God's guidance brings clarity and peace.

- **Difficulty concentrating**: One of the most immediate effects of stress is the inability to focus. A racing mind, filled with competing thoughts, makes it nearly impossible to concentrate on tasks. For example, you might find yourself sitting at your desk, staring at your to-do list, but unable to prioritize or start anything.

When this happens, consider pausing to pray and refocusing by meditating on a verse that speaks to your current situation. Philippians 4:6-7 (NIV) encourages us: *"Do not be anxious about anything, but in every situation, by prayer and petition, with thanksgiving, present your requests to God. And the peace of God, which transcends all understanding, will guard your hearts and your minds in Christ Jesus."*

- **Memory problems**: Stress affects memory by disrupting the brain's ability to store and retrieve information. This can manifest as forgetting appointments, losing track of important details, or struggling to recall something you just read. These lapses can be frustrating and erode confidence in one's abilities.

In such moments, Psalm 119:11 (NIV) reminds us of the importance of grounding ourselves in God's Word: *"I have hidden your word in my heart that I might not sin against you."* Reflecting on Scripture helps center our minds and reminds us of God's faithfulness when we feel scattered.

- **Poor decision-making**: Stress often leads to impulsive decisions or an inability to decide at all. The pressure to resolve problems quickly can cloud judgment, while fear of failure may paralyze us. For instance, you might agree to take on additional responsibilities at work despite already feeling overwhelmed, only to regret the decision later.

James 1:5 (NIV) offers guidance for these moments: *"If any of you lacks wisdom, you should ask God, who gives generously to all without finding fault, and it will be given to you."* Trusting in God's wisdom allows us to make thoughtful decisions rather than reacting out of stress or fear.

God's Perspective on Mental Strain

The Bible acknowledges our mental burdens and consistently encourages us to trust God for clarity and strength. Isaiah 26:3 (NIV) beautifully captures this promise: *"You will keep in perfect peace those whose minds are steadfast because they trust in you."*

Practical Steps for Mental Clarity in Stressful Seasons

1. **Pause and Pray**: When your thoughts feel scattered, take a moment to pray. Ask God for clarity and direction. This simple act shifts your focus from the chaos within to the peace of His presence.

2. **Meditate on Scripture**: Regularly meditating on God's Word provides an anchor for your mind. Verses like Psalm 23:3 (NIV): *"He refreshes my soul. He guides me along the right paths for His name's sake,"* reminds us of God's guidance.

3. **Break Tasks into Manageable Steps**: Overwhelm often stems from trying to do everything at once. Simplify tasks by breaking them into smaller, more achievable steps. Commit each step to God, trusting in His provision for the journey (Proverbs 16:3).

4. **Seek Wise Counsel**: When decision-making feels overwhelming, seek guidance from trusted mentors or friends who share your faith. Proverbs 15:22 (NIV) says, *"Plans fail for lack of counsel, but with many advisers, they succeed."*

5. **Rest and Reflect**: Mental clarity often comes through rest. Dedicate time to step away from the demands of life and reflect on God's promises. Jesus modeled this practice by retreating to quiet places to pray (Luke 5:16).

Embracing Peace Amid Mental Strain

While stress challenges our mental capacities, it also provides opportunities to draw closer to God. By trusting Him to guide our thoughts and decisions, we experience a peace that transcends understanding.

As you navigate seasons of mental strain, remember that God is not only your refuge but also your source of wisdom and clarity. Isaiah 40:31 (NIV) offers this encouragement: *"But those who hope in the Lord will renew their strength. They will soar on wings like eagles; they will run and not grow weary, they will walk and not be faint."*

When your mind feels overwhelmed, lean into God's strength and let His promises be the light that guides your path.

Unique Stressors for Women in Business

Women in leadership and business roles face unique challenges that amplify stress levels. These challenges stem from balancing multiple roles, societal pressures, and workplace biases. While men and women alike experience workplace stress, the specific obstacles women face often require distinct strategies for overcoming them.

As per LeanIn.org (2022), women often experience increased burnout rates due to the pressure of balancing work and family responsibilities, navigating societal norms, and addressing gender inequalities at work. As followers of Christ, women can draw strength from their faith and God's promises, finding encouragement in verses like Galatians 3:28 (NIV): *"There is neither Jew nor Greek, slave nor free, male nor female, for you are all one in Christ Jesus."*

1. The Juggling Act

Balancing a demanding career with family responsibilities often feels like an impossible task. The pressure to excel in both spheres leaves many women feeling stretched too thin, resulting in guilt, burnout, and chronic stress.

Research from **Pew Research Center (2021)** reveals that women are significantly more likely than men to report experiencing work-life conflict. For instance, a working mother juggling a crucial presentation and her children's schedules may feel conflicted between her work duties and family responsibilities, resulting in emotional fatigue.

Jesus offers solace for these burdens in Matthew 11:28-30 (NIV): *"Come to me, all you who are weary and burdened, and I will give you rest. Take my yoke upon you and learn from me, for I am gentle and humble in heart, and you will find rest for your souls."* This invitation reminds us to lean on God's strength rather than trying to bear these burdens alone.

Strategies for Managing the Juggling Act

- **Set Clear Boundaries**: Create defined work and family hours to ensure neither overlaps unnecessarily.

- **Delegate Tasks**: Enlist the support of family members or colleagues to share responsibilities.
- **Lean on God Daily**: Begin each day with prayer, asking for wisdom and balance to navigate your roles effectively.

2. Societal Expectations

Women face significant pressure to achieve a thriving career, a harmonious family, and a fulfilling personal life. Society's portrayal of the "perfect woman" fosters unrealistic expectations, leading to feelings of inadequacy, perfectionism, and self-doubt.

Clance and Imes (1978) coined the term "imposter syndrome" to describe the internalized belief of being a fraud despite evidence of success. This phenomenon disproportionately affects women, creating a cycle of overwork and burnout in an attempt to prove their worth.

God's Word provides reassurance in 2 Corinthians 12:9 (NIV): *"My grace is sufficient for you, for my power is made perfect in weakness."* This verse reminds us that God's strength compensates for our perceived shortcomings and that we don't have to strive for worldly perfection.

Strategies for Overcoming Societal Pressures

- **Redefine Success**: Align your definition of success with God's purpose for your life rather than societal standards.
- **Celebrate Small Victories**: Focus on progress over perfection, and acknowledge God's hand in your achievements.
- **Meditate on Scripture**: Reflect on verses like Psalm 139:14 (NIV): *"I praise you because I am fearfully and wonderfully made; your works are wonderful, I know that full well."*

3. Gender Bias in the Workplace

Despite advancements in gender equality, women still face challenges such as pay gaps, being overlooked for promotions, and experiencing subtle or overt discrimination. According to **McKinsey & Company (2022)**, women encounter the "broken rung" phenomenon, where they are less likely to be promoted to managerial positions than their male counterparts.

These biases create additional stress, as women feel the need to constantly prove their competence and overcome obstacles their male colleagues may not face.

In the face of these challenges, Galatians 3:28 (NIV) reminds us of our intrinsic worth in God's eyes: *"There is neither Jew nor Greek, slave nor free, male nor female, for you are all one in Christ Jesus."* This truth empowers women to view their identity through the lens of faith rather than workplace biases.

Strategies for Navigating Gender Bias

- **Build a Support Network**: Surround yourself with mentors, allies, and colleagues who advocate for equity and inclusion.

- **Communicate with Confidence**: Speak boldly about your ideas and accomplishments, knowing that your worth is rooted in God's purpose.

- **Trust God's Sovereignty**: Meditate on Joshua 1:9 (NIV): *"Have I not commanded you? Be strong and courageous. Do not be afraid; do not be discouraged, for the Lord your God will be with you wherever you go."*

Embracing Strength Through Faith

While the unique stressors women face in business are significant, they also present opportunities for growth and testimony. God equips His children with the strength, wisdom, and peace needed to overcome these challenges.

Isaiah 41:10 (NIV) offers reassurance: *"So do not fear, for I am with you; do not be dismayed, for I am your God. I will strengthen you and help you; I will uphold you with my righteous right hand."*

Through faith, intentional strategies, and reliance on God's promises, women in business can navigate these stressors with resilience and grace. Trusting in God's guidance allows them to lead confidently, embracing their God-given potential and purpose.

Mindfulness: A Christian Perspective

Mindfulness, often associated with secular wellness practices, takes on profound significance when viewed through a biblical lens. For Christians, mindfulness is not merely about being present in the moment; it is about intentionally focusing on God's presence, acknowledging His sovereignty, and inviting Him into every aspect of our lives. This Christ-centered mindfulness aligns our hearts and minds with His will, allowing us to experience the peace that surpasses all understanding, grounding us in His truth and presence.

Philippians 4:6-7 (NIV) beautifully illustrates this practice: *"Do not be anxious about anything, but in every situation, by prayer and petition, with thanksgiving, present your requests to God. And the peace of God, which transcends all understanding, will guard your hearts and your minds in Christ Jesus."* This passage reminds us that true mindfulness comes from surrendering our worries to God, trusting Him to guide us, and finding peace in His presence.

Mindfulness for Christian women goes beyond simple relaxation techniques. It becomes a spiritual discipline that deepens our relationship with God, strengthens our faith, and brings clarity to our lives.

The following are three key aspects of mindfulness from a Christian perspective:

- **Prayer pauses**: In the busyness of life, it is easy to let the demands of the day overshadow our connection with God. Prayer pauses involve taking intentional moments throughout the day to step back, breathe deeply, and commune with Him.

For example, before beginning a challenging task, you might pause to pray:

"Lord, guide my thoughts and actions as I face this challenge. Help me to rely on Your wisdom and not my own understanding."

Jesus modeled this practice of pausing to pray during His ministry. Luke 5:16 (NIV) says, *"But Jesus often withdrew to lonely places and prayed."* These intentional pauses allow us to recalibrate our focus, shifting it from our worries to God's promises.

- **Scripture meditation**: Meditating on God's Word anchors our thoughts in His truths, providing perspective and reassurance in the face of stress or uncertainty. Reflecting on Scripture not only calms our minds but also fortifies our spirits with God's promises.

Consider Psalm 119:105 (NIV): *"Your word is a lamp to my feet and a light for my path."* This verse reminds us that Scripture illuminates our path, guiding us through life's challenges and providing comfort in times of uncertainty.

Practical steps for Scripture meditation:

- Choose a verse that resonates with your current situation.

- Read it slowly and repeatedly, letting its meaning sink into your heart.

- Pray over the verse, asking God to reveal how it applies to your life.

- **Present-moment focus**: Engaging fully in the present moment becomes an act of worship when done with an awareness of God's presence. Whether completing a work project, spending time with family, or enjoying a quiet moment of reflection, being fully present honors God and shows gratitude for His gifts.

Colossians 3:23 (NIV) encourages us: *"Whatever you do, work at it with all your heart, as working for the Lord, not for human masters."* This verse highlights that ordinary activities become spiritually meaningful when carried out with a heart devoted to worship.

Practical ways to practice present-moment focus:

- Before starting a task, dedicate it to God in prayer.

- Avoid multitasking; give your full attention to one thing at a time.

- Acknowledge God's presence in every situation, thanking Him for His guidance and provision.

Benefits of Christian Mindfulness

When we embrace mindfulness through a biblical perspective, we invite God's peace and wisdom into our daily lives. The benefits extend beyond spiritual growth to our mental and emotional well-being:

- **Reduced Anxiety:** When we entrust our concerns to God and center our thoughts on His presence, we find solace from anxiety and fear (1 Peter 5:7).

- **Enhanced Clarity:** Consistent prayer and meditation assist us in understanding God's intentions, empowering us to make sound choices.

- **Strengthened Relationships**: Being fully present with loved ones fosters deeper connections and reflects Christ's love.

- **Greater Resilience:** Rooted in God's assurances, we confront obstacles with bravery and trust.

Incorporating God in Daily Mindfulness Practices

Mindfulness, when rooted in Christ, transforms how we navigate life's complexities. It is not about perfection but about prioritizing God's presence in every moment. As Isaiah 26:3 (NIV) assures us, "You *will keep in perfect peace those whose minds are steadfast, because they trust in you."*

Each day presents an opportunity to practice mindfulness through:

1. **Morning Reflection**: Begin the day with prayer and Scripture, setting the tone for mindful awareness of God's presence.

2. **Midday Pauses**: Take breaks to reconnect with God, asking for strength and guidance.

3. **Evening Gratitude**: End the day by reflecting on God's blessings and surrendering any lingering worries to Him.

Embrace mindfulness through a Christian lens to discover the peace, clarity, and strength that come from walking closely with the Lord, guiding you through life's challenges with His unwavering love. Let this practice guide you deeper into His presence, where true rest and renewal await. Let this practice draw you deeper into His presence, where true rest and renewal are found.

CHAPTER 2

THE UNSEEN WEIGHT OF STRESS

Stress isn't just a fleeting reaction to a single challenge; it is an all-encompassing experience that quietly infiltrates every part of our lives. It can be as subtle as a persistent feeling of unease or as overwhelming as a physical and emotional breakdown. Its full impact is often unnoticed until it leads to physical and emotional exhaustion, persistent feelings of frustration, or overwhelming hopelessness.

Life's demands may seem relentless—juggling the responsibilities of a demanding career, nurturing family relationships, managing finances, and striving for personal growth. Yet, even in our most burdened moments, the Word of God offers a comforting reminder: we are not alone. Isaiah 41:10 (NIV) reassures us:

"Do not fear, for I am with you; do not be dismayed, for I am your God. I will strengthen you and help you; I will uphold you with my righteous right hand."

This divine promise reminds us that God is fully aware of our burdens. He not only sees our struggles but also offers His strength and support to sustain us through them.

Stress affects us physically, emotionally, and mentally. Its presence may not always be obvious, but its effects can be profound and far-reaching. Understanding these stress layers is crucial for effectively overcoming them.

1. Physical Manifestations of Stress

Our bodies are designed to respond to stress through the "fight or flight" mechanism. Although this response is essential in dangerous situations, modern life can prolong its activation beyond its intended purpose. The result is often physical strain and discomfort that affects overall well-being.

Common physical effects of stress include:

- **Sleep disturbances**: Tossing and turning at night due to racing thoughts or lingering worries. Chronic sleep deprivation exacerbates stress, leaving us mentally foggy and emotionally drained. Jesus invites us to find true rest in Him, saying in Matthew 11:28 (NIV): *"Come to me, all you who are weary and burdened, and I will give you rest."*

- **Weakened immunity**: Prolonged stress suppresses the immune system, increasing vulnerability to illnesses such as colds, flu, or infections (Cohen et al., 2007).

- **Muscle tension and pain**: Stress often manifests in tight shoulders, a clenched jaw, or backaches, which are physical reminders of internal struggles.

- **Digestive issues**: The gut is highly sensitive to stress, which can lead to nausea, bloating, or irritable bowel syndrome (Mayer, 2011).

- **Heart health risks**: Chronic stress elevates blood pressure and heart rate, increasing the risk of cardiovascular problems (American Heart Association, 2019).

During times of stress, it's essential to pause and recall God's care for us. Psalm 29:11 (NIV) reminds us: *"The Lord gives strength to His people; the Lord blesses His people with peace."*

2. Emotional Turmoil

Stress also damages our emotions, creating a rollercoaster of emotions that can be difficult to navigate. Women, in particular, often bear the emotional load of nurturing and caregiving while striving to meet personal and professional demands.

Emotional symptoms of stress include:

- **Anxiety and worry**: A constant sense of unease that overshadows moments of peace.

- **Irritability**: A shorter temper that can strain relationships with loved ones or colleagues.

- **Feelings of overwhelm**: A sense of drowning in responsibilities, leading to tears, withdrawal, or even emotional shutdown.

- **Hopelessness**: A prolonged state of sadness or loss of motivation that saps joy and purpose.

Finding solace in God's Word is crucial during emotional turmoil. Psalm 34:18 (NIV) offers this assurance: *"The Lord is close to the brokenhearted and saves those who are crushed in spirit."* In these moments, His nearness becomes our refuge and source of healing.

3. Mental Strain

The mental toll of stress is perhaps the most insidious. It impacts how we think, process information, and make decisions. Stress can cloud our minds and make simple tasks feel overwhelming.

Cognitive effects of stress include:

- **Difficulty concentrating**: A racing mind struggles to focus, jumping from one thought to another without resolution.
- **Memory problems**: Forgetting important details or appointments due to mental clutter.
- **Impaired decision-making**: Stress can lead to impulsive choices or paralysis when faced with too many options.

Proverbs 3:5-6 (NIV) offers wisdom for moments of mental fog: *"Trust in the Lord with all your heart and lean not on your own understanding; in all your ways submit to Him, and He will make your paths straight."* Surrendering our thoughts and plans to God allows Him to bring clarity and direction in our decision-making process.

Lifting the Weight: Faith-Centered Strategies

In this section, you will explore faith-centered strategies for navigating stress with resilience and grace.

Stress may be unavoidable, but it is not unmanageable. Christians have access to spiritual tools and practical steps that enable us to face stress with resilience and grace.

1. Lay Your Burdens at His Feet

Jesus invites us to cast our worries on Him. In Matthew 11:28–30 (NIV), He promises rest for the weary. Begin each day with prayer, surrendering your anxieties to God and asking for His strength to guide you.

2. Practice Intentional Rest

Rest is not laziness; it is obedience to God's design. Psalm 23:2-3 (NIV) beautifully depicts His desire for us to find renewal: *"He makes me lie down in green pastures, He leads me beside quiet waters, He refreshes my soul."* Set aside time each day to step away from the noise and reflect on His goodness.

3. Seek Wisdom Through Scripture

God's Word is a source of strength and clarity. Meditate on verses like Isaiah 26:3 (NIV): *"You will keep in perfect peace those whose minds are steadfast, because they trust in you."* Let Scripture be the anchor that steadies your thoughts and guides your decisions.

4. Build a Support Network

Surround yourself with trusted friends, mentors, or a church community that can offer encouragement and accountability. Proverbs 27:17 (NIV) says, *"As iron sharpens iron, so one person sharpens another."*

5. Incorporate Healthy Habits

Nurture your body with proper nutrition, exercise, and sleep. These practical steps honor the temple of the Holy Spirit and equip you to handle stress more effectively (1 Corinthians 6:19-20).

Conclusion: Anchored in His Peace

The weight of stress may touch every corner of our lives, but it does not have to define us. God's presence offers hope, His Word provides clarity, and His peace sustains us.

As you navigate the challenges of stress, take heart in the words of John 14:27 (NIV): *"Peace I leave with you; my peace I give you. I do not give to you as the world gives. Do not let your hearts be troubled and do not be afraid."*

Let this chapter remind you that stress is not your master—Christ is. In Him, you will find the strength, peace, and resilience needed to face life's pressures with confidence and joy.

Navigating Stress with Grace and Faith

Stress is a reality we all face, but as followers of Christ, we are not called to endure it alone. God's Word reassures us that He is with us in every trial, equipping us with the tools and strength to navigate life's pressures with resilience and grace. Stress, when surrendered to God, can become an opportunity for spiritual growth and deeper reliance on His promises.

1. Surrender Your Burdens

The first step to managing stress is recognizing that we cannot carry it alone. Jesus invites us to place our burdens at His feet and entrust

Him with the weight we carry. Matthew 11:28-30 (NIV) offers this powerful promise:

"Come to me, all you who are weary and burdened, and I will give you rest. Take my yoke upon you and learn from me, for I am gentle and humble in heart, and you will find rest for your souls. For my yoke is easy and my burden is light."

To surrender our burdens is to acknowledge that God is sovereign and capable of handling what feels overwhelming. Begin each day in prayer, offering your worries to Him:

"Lord, I give You my anxieties and challenges today. Help me trust in Your plan and rest in Your strength."

Practical Application:

- Write down the specific worries or tasks that feel unmanageable.
- Pray over each one, asking God to take control and provide wisdom.
- Let go of the need to solve everything immediately, trusting His timing.

2. Practice Mindful Prayer

Mindful prayer is a practice of turning our focus from the chaos around us to the peace of God's presence. It allows us to pause, breathe deeply, and realign our thoughts with His truths. Philippians 4:6-7 (NIV) encourages us:

"Do not be anxious about anything, but in every situation, by prayer and petition, with thanksgiving, present your requests to God. And the peace

of God, which transcends all understanding, will guard your hearts and your minds in Christ Jesus."

Mindful prayer can transform moments of stress into opportunities for connection with God. For example, in a tense meeting or while juggling family demands, take a few seconds to silently pray:

"Lord, calm my heart and guide my thoughts. Help me focus on Your presence and respond with grace."

Practical Application:

- Set reminders to pray throughout your day, especially during stressful moments.
- Practice deep breathing while meditating on Scripture, such as Psalm 46:10 (NIV): *"Be still, and know that I am God."*
- Keep a journal to document prayers and reflect on how God answers them.

3. Seek Godly Wisdom

Stress often clouds our judgment, making it difficult to discern the best course of action. In these moments, turning to God's Word provides clarity and assurance. Proverbs 16:3 (NIV) reminds us:

"Commit to the Lord whatever you do, and He will establish your plans."

When faced with difficult decisions or overwhelming tasks, take time to pray for wisdom. James 1:5 (NIV) offers this encouragement:

"If any of you lacks wisdom, you should ask God, who gives generously to all without finding fault, and it will be given to you."

Practical Application:

- Before making decisions, spend time reading Scripture related to the situation.

- Seek counsel from trusted Christian mentors or friends. Proverbs 11:14 (NIV) says, *"For lack of guidance a nation falls, but victory is won through many advisers."*

- Ask God to align your desires and plans with His will, trusting Him to guide your steps.

4. Rest in His Presence

Rest is not just a physical necessity; it is a spiritual discipline. God designed rest as a way to renew our bodies, minds, and souls. Psalm 23:2-3 (NIV) beautifully depicts the restorative nature of God's care: *"He makes me lie down in green pastures, He leads me beside quiet waters, He refreshes my soul."*

In a world that values busyness, prioritizing rest intentionally becomes an act of faith. It acknowledges that God is in control, even when we step back to recharge.

Practical Application:

- Schedule regular times in your week for rest and reflection. These could include a Sabbath day or moments of quiet each evening.

- Spend time in nature, appreciating God's creation as a way to reconnect with Him.

- Use rest as an opportunity to meditate on Scripture, journaling thoughts and prayers as you reflect on His goodness.

The Peace of God: Our Anchor Amid Stress

In the midst of life's storms, God's peace becomes our unshakable anchor, guiding us through every trial with unwavering strength and assurance.

Navigating stress with grace and faith does not guarantee that we will never feel overwhelmed. However, it does mean that in every trial, we have access to God's peace, strength, and guidance. His promises anchor us, reminding us that we are never alone.

Jesus offers this reassurance in John 14:27 (NIV):

"Peace I leave with you; my peace I give you. I do not give to you as the world gives. Do not let your hearts be troubled and do not be afraid."

By surrendering our burdens, practicing mindful prayer, seeking godly wisdom, and resting in His presence, we can face life's pressures with renewed strength and confidence. Let this be a reminder that stress does not define us—God's grace does.

Closing Prayer:

Lord, thank You for being our refuge in times of stress. Help us surrender our burdens to You, seek Your wisdom, and rest in Your presence. May Your peace, which transcends all understanding, guard our hearts and minds as we navigate life's challenges. Amen.

Conclusion: Anchored in His Peace

Stress may touch every corner of our existence, but it does not have to define us. It is not the burdens of life that overwhelm us, but how we carry them. As followers of Christ, we are invited to let go of the weight we were never meant to bear and trust in God's sustaining power.

John 14:27 (NIV) beautifully captures Jesus's assurance: *"Peace I leave with you; my peace I give you. I do not give to you as the world gives. Do not let your hearts be troubled, and do not be afraid."* Peace is not temporary or reliant on situations; it's a lasting, divine gift beyond comprehension.

When we choose to lean into God's promises, we find clarity amidst confusion, strength in our weaknesses, and peace that guards our hearts and minds. Stress may challenge us, but it also serves as an opportunity to draw closer to God, relying on His wisdom and grace to guide us through.

Living Anchored in His Peace

To live anchored in God's peace, we must intentionally prioritize His presence in our lives:

1. **Begin Each Day with Him**: We should start our mornings in prayer and reflection, surrendering the day's challenges to God.

2. **Meditate on His Word**: Let Scripture be your anchor, reminding you of His promises when stress arises. Verses like Philippians 4:6-7 (NIV) encourage us: *"Do not be anxious about anything, but in every situation, by prayer and petition, with thanksgiving, present your requests to God. And the peace of God, which transcends all understanding, will guard your hearts and your minds in Christ Jesus."*

3. **Rest in His Presence**: Throughout your day, create moments of stillness to reconnect with God and let His peace renew your spirit.

Trusting Him Through Every Trial

Sharing a personal reflection on trusting God in the midst of trials, you can attest to the transformative power of faith and reliance on His guidance.

God's peace helps us navigate life's challenges confidently, clearly, and joyfully. Isaiah 41:10 (NIV) reassures us: *"Do not fear, for I am with you; do not be dismayed, for I am your God. I will strengthen you and help you; I will uphold you with my righteous right hand."*

As you journey through **life's pressures**, remember that God's presence goes before you, His promises sustain you in every moment, and His peace surrounds you continually. Whatever stress you face, you are not alone—He is your refuge, your strength, and your source of unshakable calm.

Let this chapter be a foundation for embracing God's peace in the midst of stress. Being anchored in God's love and faithfulness provides a steady foundation for navigating life's trials with grace. His love reassures us that we are never alone, even in our most difficult moments. As Romans 8:38-39 (NIV) reminds us: *"For I am convinced that neither death nor life, neither angels nor demons, neither the present nor the future, nor any powers, neither height nor depth, nor anything else in all creation, will be able to separate us from the love of God that is in Christ Jesus our Lord."* This unshakable truth gives us the confidence to confront challenges without fear, assured that His love envelops and supports us.

God's faithfulness, on the other hand, assures us that He keeps His promises and will never forsake us. Lamentations 3:22-23 (NIV) declares: *"Because of the Lord's great love we are not consumed, for His compassions never fail. They are new every morning; great is Your faithfulness."* In moments of trials, this faithfulness becomes our beacon of hope. We can trust that His plans are good and His timing is perfect, even when our circumstances feel overwhelming.

Being anchored in His love and faithfulness transforms the way we approach trials:

1. **It Provides Peace Amidst Chaos**: Knowing that God's love is constant allows us to remain calm and centered, even when life feels chaotic. As Isaiah 26:3 (NIV) promises, "You *will keep in perfect peace those whose minds are steadfast, because they trust in You."*

2. **It Strengthens Us for the Journey**: God's faithfulness equips us with the courage and resilience to keep moving forward. Philippians 4:13 (NIV) reminds us: *"I can do all this through Him who gives me strength."*

3. **It Inspires Graceful Responses**: Anchored in His love, we are empowered to respond to challenges with grace, reflecting His kindness and compassion in our actions and attitudes.

When we are anchored in God's love and faithfulness, our trials become opportunities to grow in faith, demonstrate His character, and experience His peace in ways that defy worldly understanding. With Him as our anchor, we can not just survive but thrive, coming out of life's challenges stronger, wiser, and more grounded in His presence.

CHAPTER 3

THE SYNERGY OF FAITH AND MINDFULNESS IN THE LIVES OF CHRISTIAN BUSINESSWOMEN

In the demanding lives of Christian businesswomen, integrating faith and mindfulness offers a transformative approach to navigating challenges, fostering spiritual growth, and achieving professional excellence.

Reflecting on scriptures such as *"Be still, and know that I am God"* (Psalm 46:10, NIV) and *"Do not worry about tomorrow"* (Matthew 6:34, NIV) reveals timeless truths that encourage mindfulness and reliance on God. These principles empower women to approach their responsibilities with calmness, clarity, and resilience, transforming high-pressure situations into opportunities to glorify God.

Historical Context and Biblical Roots of Mindfulness

Mindfulness is commonly associated with Eastern philosophies; however, its origins are firmly rooted in biblical teachings and early Christian traditions. At its core, mindfulness is being present and intentional, a concept that echoes throughout Scripture and the spiritual disciplines of early Christian communities.

Historical Context

The Bible was written in cultural contexts where stillness, prayer, and reflection were central to spiritual life. Ancient Hebrew practices focused on reflecting deeply on God's Word to understand His truths and align one's heart with His will. Psalm 1:2 (NIV) captures this beautifully:

"...whose delight is in the law of the Lord, and who meditates on his law day and night."

This call to constant meditation on God's Word reflects a deliberate concentration on His presence and guidance. Such practices were not just spiritual exercises but ways of life, fostering a continuous awareness of God in every moment.

The Desert Fathers and Early Monastic Traditions

Early Christian monastics, such as the Desert Fathers of the 3rd and 4th centuries, modeled mindfulness through solitude, prayer, and introspection. These hermits and monks withdrew to the desert to cultivate an unbroken awareness of God's presence, integrating practices like contemplative prayer and *lectio divina* (divine reading).

Lectio Divina is a form of meditative Scripture reading that involves reading the Bible slowly and prayerfully, allowing God's Word to resonate deeply. As noted by Keating in 2008, this practice closely resembles modern mindfulness techniques by emphasizing focus, reflection, and intentionality.

Biblical Commands for Stillness

The Bible repeatedly calls believers to stillness as a way to experience God's peace. Psalm 46:10 (NIV) instructs:
"Be still, and know that I am God."

In today's fast-paced world, this call to stillness is as relevant as ever. It invites Christians to pause amidst the chaos and reconnect with God. This principle of intentional quietness aligns with the essence of mindfulness, reminding believers that peace is found in God's presence.

Scholarly Connections

Modern theological and psychological research further highlights the synergy between mindfulness and biblical principles.

Dr. Thomas Keating

A Trappist monk and spiritual teacher, Dr. Thomas Keating emphasized the integration of mindfulness within Christian spirituality. In his work on centering prayer, Keating draws from Psalm 46:10, emphasizing stillness as a means of deepening one's connection with

God. This practice involves quieting the mind and focusing on God's presence, fostering both spiritual and emotional well-being.

The Journal of Psychology and Christianity

Contemporary studies published in *The Journal of Psychology and Christianity* explore the impact of Christian mindfulness on emotional health. Kabat-Zinn (2013) identifies overlaps between mindfulness techniques and biblical teachings, particularly in fostering resilience, reducing anxiety, and cultivating peace. These findings underscore how mindfulness, when rooted in Scripture, enhances spiritual growth and mental clarity.

Jesus' Teachings on Mindfulness

Jesus consistently highlighted the significance of living in the present moment and having faith in God at all times. His teachings provide valuable guidance on how to practice mindfulness grounded in faith in everyday life.

Trust in God's Provision

In Matthew 6:28-34 (NIV), Jesus encourages His followers to release worry about the future:

"Consider the lilies of the field, how they grow. They do not labor or spin. Yet I tell you that not even Solomon in all his splendor was dressed like one of these... Do not worry about tomorrow, for tomorrow will worry about itself."

This teaching aligns with mindfulness principles by redirecting attention from future anxieties to present blessings. Jesus' words remind believers to trust God's provision and focus on His presence in the present.

The Good Samaritan: Attentiveness to Others

In the parable of the Good Samaritan (Luke 10:25–37), Jesus highlights the importance of being fully present to the needs of others. Unlike the priest and Levite, who were preoccupied and hurried, the Samaritan demonstrated mindfulness through attentiveness and compassion.

This story encourages Christian businesswomen to approach their work and relationships with the same intentionality and care, embodying Christ's love in every interaction.

Relevance for Christian Businesswomen

Understanding the historical and biblical roots of mindfulness offers Christian businesswomen a meaningful way to align their faith with their professional and personal lives. This integration is far from a modern or secular adaptation—it is a practice deeply rooted in God's Word. By embracing mindfulness through a Christian lens, women can cultivate clarity, emotional resilience, and spiritual growth, equipping them to navigate challenges with grace and purpose.

Practical Applications

- **Meditate on Scripture**: Scripture meditation is a powerful way to center your thoughts on God's truths and promises. Reflecting on verses like Philippians 4:6-7 (NIV) helps redirect anxieties toward trust in God:

> *"Do not be anxious about anything, but in every situation, by prayer and petition, with thanksgiving, present your requests to God. And the peace of God, which transcends all understanding, will guard your hearts and your minds in Christ Jesus."*

How to Practice:

- **Practice Stillness**: In the busyness of professional life, taking intentional moments of stillness allows you to reconnect with God. This practice aligns with Psalm 46:10 (NIV): *"Be still, and know that I am God."* Stillness is not just physical quietness but also a spiritual posture of surrender and attentiveness.

How to Practice:

- **Cultivate Gratitude**: Gratitude shifts focus from worries to blessings, helping to cultivate a positive and faith-filled mindset. Jesus modeled gratitude throughout His ministry, even in challenging circumstances, reminding us to appreciate God's provision in the present moment.

How to Practice:

The Impact of Mindfulness on Christian Businesswomen

By weaving these faith-based mindfulness practices into their routines, Christian businesswomen can:

1. **Navigate Challenges with Clarity**: Engaging in scripture meditation and moments of stillness offers valuable wisdom and perspective during stressful times.

2. **Maintain Emotional Balance**: Gratitude and trust in God foster peace, reducing anxiety and burnout.
3. **Reflect God's Love**: Mindfulness creates space for intentional, compassionate interactions, allowing His love to shine through their actions.

As they integrate these practices, they grow spiritually and exemplify faith in action, inspiring colleagues, clients, and communities with their grace and purpose-driven leadership.

In conclusion, the synergy of faith and mindfulness equips Christian businesswomen to navigate life with clarity, purpose, and peace, aligning professional excellence with spiritual growth and transforming every moment into an act of worship and trust in God's unwavering faithfulness.

Mindfulness, when rooted in Scripture, is a gift that aligns with God's design for our lives. It equips Christian businesswomen to focus on His presence, embrace His peace, and approach their work and relationships with renewed confidence and trust. By anchoring their lives in His truths, they become living examples of His love and wisdom, bringing light to the world around them.

Biblical Foundations of Mindfulness

Mindfulness, when rooted in Scripture, invites believers to focus intentionally on God's presence, release their anxieties, and trust in His unwavering guidance. This practice transforms how we approach life's challenges, shifting our focus from worldly worries to divine peace. Philippians 4:6-7 (NIV) beautifully encapsulates this principle:

"Do not be anxious about anything, but in every situation, by prayer and petition, with thanksgiving, present your requests to God. And the peace

of God, which transcends all understanding, will guard your hearts and your minds in Christ Jesus."

This verse reminds us that mindfulness, grounded in faith, involves surrendering our burdens to God and embracing the peace He provides—a peace that surpasses all human comprehension.

Practical Applications of Biblical Mindfulness

- **Pause to Pray**: Prayer serves as a powerful tool for regaining focus and finding peace in the midst of chaos. Taking a moment to pray before a high-stress situation or critical decision can transform anxiety into trust and fear into peace.

How to Practice:

- **Reflect on Scripture**: Meditating on Scripture throughout the day anchors our hearts and minds in God's truth. Verses like Psalm 46:10 (NIV)—*"Be still, and know that I am God"*—offer a reminder to pause and acknowledge His sovereignty, even amidst the busiest schedules.

How to Practice:

- **Follow Jesus' Example of Mindfulness:** Throughout His ministry, Jesus demonstrated mindfulness, showing unwavering attentiveness and compassion in His interactions. Whether He was healing the sick, teaching multitudes, or sharing bread with His disciples, He was fully present in every moment.

One of the most profound examples of this is found in the parable of the Good Samaritan (Luke 10:25–37). In the story, the Samaritan notices and responds to the needs of an injured man, while others pass by preoccupied with their own concerns. This attentiveness and compassion illustrate the essence of biblical mindfulness: seeing and serving others with love and intentionality.

Jesus modeled mindfulness in His ministry. Whether healing the sick or sharing parables, He was fully present. His attentiveness in the parable of the Good Samaritan (Luke 10:25–37) inspires us to notice and respond to others with compassion and intentionality.

The Transformative Power of Biblical Mindfulness

Mindfulness rooted in Scripture is not just a tool for reducing stress; it is a spiritual discipline that deepens our relationship with God and enriches our interactions with others. By pausing to pray, reflecting on His Word, and following Jesus' example, we create space for God's peace to reign in our hearts and guide our actions.

As Colossians 3:15 (NIV) reminds us:

"Let the peace of Christ rule in your hearts, since as members of one body you were called to peace. And be thankful."

When we incorporate biblical mindfulness into our daily lives, we embrace this peace and allow it to transform our responses to life's challenges. This fosters a spirit of gratitude, compassion, and trust in God's perfect plan.

Prayer as a Tool for Stress Relief

Dive deeper into the benefits of prayer for stress management, explore various prayer techniques such as breath prayers or gratitude prayers, and discuss how prayer can positively impact mental and emotional well-being during challenging situations.

Prayer is not just a spiritual discipline; it is a lifeline that connects us to God's presence, providing peace and clarity in the midst of life's challenges. It serves as a form of mindfulness, shifting our focus from stress to trust in God's sovereignty. Psalm 55:22 (NIV) captures this invitation beautifully:

"Cast your cares on the Lord, and he will sustain you; he will never let the righteous be shaken."

By casting our cares on Him, we are reminded that we don't have to bear life's burdens alone. Prayer transforms instances of anxiety into opportunities to experience God's sustaining grace and peace.

Personal Renewal Through Prayer

Prayer profoundly impacts our mental, emotional, and physical well-being. It allows us to pause, breathe, and align our thoughts with God's truths, reducing the weight of our worries.

Practical Example: Imagine a businesswoman facing a challenging negotiation scenario. By pausing for a moment of prayer and trusting in God's guidance, she can approach the situation with a calm and confident demeanor, reflecting the principles of mindfulness and faith in action.

Imagine a businesswoman preparing for a high-stakes presentation. Anxiety begins to creep in, clouding her focus. She takes a moment to pray, *"Lord, grant me wisdom and courage. Help me to rely on Your strength and not my own."*

This simple yet heartfelt prayer shifts her mindset, reminding her that she is not alone in her efforts. Studies from the **American Psychological Association (2015)** indicate that prayer can lower stress hormones, reduce blood pressure, and promote a sense of calm. It serves as a practical and spiritual way to regulate emotions and restore clarity.

Gratitude in Prayer

Gratitude is a transformative aspect of prayer that redirects our focus from worries to blessings. When we thank God for His provision, even in challenging circumstances, we foster resilience and deepen our faith.

Practical Example:

A woman facing financial uncertainty might pray, "Thank *You, Lord, for the opportunities You've given me and the strength to persevere through this season."* By expressing gratitude, she shifts her perspective from fear of lack to trust in God's abundant provision.

Gratitude in prayer aligns with 1 Thessalonians 5:18 (NIV): *"Give thanks in all circumstances; for this is God's will for you in Christ Jesus."* This verse reminds us that God's faithfulness is unwavering, even in difficulties.

The Dual Impact of Prayer

Prayer is both a spiritual refuge and a practical tool for managing stress. It calms our hearts, clears our minds, and reaffirms our trust in God's promises. By incorporating personal renewal and gratitude into prayer, we infuse God's peace into every area of our lives.

Philippians 4:6-7 (NIV) assures us of the power of prayer:

"Do not be anxious about anything, but in every situation, by prayer and petition, with thanksgiving, present your requests to God. And the peace of God, which transcends all understanding, will guard your hearts and your minds in Christ Jesus."

Through prayer, we find the strength to navigate challenges, the wisdom to make sound decisions, and the peace that only God can provide. It becomes a tool not just for stress relief but for living a life anchored in His presence and grace.

Integrating Faith into Daily Life

Consider how starting each day with prayer and scripture can shape decision-making, help us reflect on God's promises during challenging moments, and encourage us to approach work with a mindset of serving God in all endeavors.

Integrating faith into daily tasks transforms them into opportunities for worship, aligning actions with God's purpose. Proverbs 16:3 (NIV) encourages: *"Commit to the Lord whatever you do, and he will establish your plans."*

Beginning each day with prayer and scripture sets a foundation of clarity and peace. Reflecting on Lamentations 3:22-23 (NIV)—*"Because of the Lord's great love we are not consumed, for his compassions never fail. They are new every morning; great is your faithfulness"*—reminds us of God's fresh mercies and faithfulness.

Faith shapes professional conduct, fostering excellence and integrity. Colossians 3:23 (NIV) inspires: *"Whatever you do, work at it with all your heart, as working for the Lord, not for human masters."* Approaching tasks with this mindset makes even mundane duties meaningful.

For instance, prior to facilitating a difficult team meeting, a Christian businesswoman could seek wisdom through prayer (James 1:5, NIV) and contemplate handling the situation with grace and empathy.

Building Faithful Habits

To deepen your spiritual connection, consider incorporating scripture meditation at specific times of the day, journaling prayers for reflection, seeking community and accountability for support, and finding moments of gratitude in everyday activities.

Faith grows through consistent practices that integrate spirituality into daily routines.

- **Scripture Meditation**: During lunch breaks, reflect on verses like Philippians 4:13 (NIV): *"I can do all this through him who gives me strength."*
- **Journaling Prayers**: At the end of the day, write down prayers of gratitude and reflection to strengthen your connection with God.

Community and Accountability

Community provides strength and encouragement. Proverbs 27:17 (NIV) says: *"As iron sharpens iron, so one person sharpens another."*

Mentorship and Accountability

Mentorship fosters spiritual and professional growth. Accountability partners provide prayer support and help women align their priorities with God's Word. For instance, a businesswoman navigating ethical challenges may find guidance and prayerful support in a mentor.

Finding God in the Everyday

Faith thrives in ordinary moments. Whispering a prayer of gratitude while preparing meals or reflecting on God's blessings during a commute transforms routine tasks into worship.

Matthew 5:16 (NIV) reminds us: *"Let your light shine before others, that they may see your good deeds and glorify your Father in heaven."* By integrating faith into every aspect of life, Christian women demonstrate God's love and grace, turning challenges into opportunities to glorify Him.

In conclusion, the synergy of faith and mindfulness equips Christian businesswomen to navigate life with clarity, purpose, and peace, aligning professional excellence with spiritual growth and transforming every moment into an act of worship and trust in God's unwavering faithfulness.

The synergy of faith and mindfulness equips Christian businesswomen to navigate life with clarity, purpose, and peace. Rooted in biblical principles, these practices provide a framework for aligning professional excellence with spiritual growth, transforming every moment into an act of worship and trust in God's unwavering faithfulness.

CHAPTER 4

EMBRACING THE PRESENT MOMENT

Embracing the present moment is both a challenge and a necessity in a world that encourages constant multitasking and thrives on distractions. For Christian businesswomen, this practice goes beyond mindfulness; it becomes a deliberate act of faith, anchoring life in God's presence.

This chapter offers practical tools, such as deep breathing exercises, mindful walking techniques, journaling prompts, and gratitude practices, to help women navigate life's complexities. These practices empower women to balance their spiritual lives and professional responsibilities, foster meaningful relationships, and approach challenges with grace.

The Power of Now

Living in the present moment—often referred to as "The Power of Now"—is not merely a concept but a transformative practice for Christian businesswomen. It provides an anchor of clarity and peace in the midst of life's relentless demands, releasing the weight of past regrets and the grip of future anxieties. This practice invites a deep sense of purpose, grounded in the blessings and opportunities that God has placed before us today.

A Spiritual Discipline, Not Just Mindfulness

For Christian women, living in the present is more than a mindfulness technique; it is a profound spiritual discipline. It means intentionally seeking and experiencing God's presence in every moment, recognizing that He is actively working in our lives. Philippians 4:6-7 (NIV) offers a guiding principle for this practice:

"Do not be anxious about anything, but in every situation, by prayer and petition, with thanksgiving, present your requests to God. And the peace of God, which transcends all understanding, will guard your hearts and your minds in Christ Jesus."

This verse from Philippians 4:6-7 shows us that peace doesn't come from perfect circumstances but is a gift from God when we entrust our worries to Him. It reminds us to approach every moment with gratitude, intentional prayer, and unwavering faith.

Why "The Power of Now" Matters for Christian Businesswomen

Meetings, deadlines, and decisions can easily overwhelm our minds in the business world. The future looms with uncertainties, while past mistakes can weigh heavily on our hearts. However, *The Power of Now* invites us to step away from this cycle, trust in God's plan, and embrace the present as a sacred opportunity to align with His will.

Example of Trusting the Present

A businesswoman preparing for a critical presentation might feel anxiety creeping in, tempted to replay past failures or obsess over future outcomes. Instead, she pauses, breathes deeply, and prays:

"Lord, grant me wisdom and calmness. Thank You for the opportunity to serve You through my work. Help me focus on what I can do in this moment and leave the rest in Your hands."

Scriptural Insights on Living in the Present

The Bible is replete with reminders of God's call to live fully in the present, trusting Him to handle the past and future.

1. **Matthew 6:34 (NIV):** *"Therefore do not worry about tomorrow, for tomorrow will worry about itself. Each day has enough trouble of its own."*
   Jesus encourages us to release the burden of the future, focusing instead on what we can do today.

Practical Example:

A woman juggling work and family might feel overwhelmed by tomorrow's demands. However, by focusing on one task at a time and trusting God to guide her steps, she can navigate her day with grace and intention.

1. **Isaiah 26:3 (NIV):** *"You will keep in perfect peace those whose minds are steadfast because they trust in you."*
   This verse from Isaiah 26:3 promises that steadfast trust in God brings peace, helping us remain grounded and calm, even in chaotic circumstances.

Practical Applications of "The Power of Now"

1. Pause to Pray

Taking intentional moments to pause and pray throughout the day is a powerful way to refocus on God's presence.

Example:

Before a challenging conversation, whisper a quick prayer:

"Lord, guide my words and actions. Help me reflect Your love and wisdom in this moment."

This act of surrender transforms nervousness into trust, allowing God's peace to calm your spirit.

2. Gratitude in the Present

Practiced gratitude shifts our focus from what we lack to the abundance of God's blessings.

Example:

At the end of a stressful day, take a moment to thank God for the small victories—a kind word from a colleague, the strength to meet deadlines, or the beauty of a sunset. Reflect on James 1:17 (NIV):

"Every good and perfect gift is from above."

Gratitude not only lifts the spirit but also reinforces faith in God's provision.

3. Engaging Fully in Relationships

Being present in our relationships demonstrates Christ's love and care.

Example:

When speaking with a team member or family member, set aside distractions and listen attentively. Reflect on Ephesians 4:2 (NIV):

"Be completely humble and gentle; be patient, bearing with one another in love."

This practice not only strengthens connections but also creates opportunities to reflect God's grace in everyday interactions.

The Spiritual Power of Now

Living in the present moment is a profound act of worship. It demonstrates trust in God's control and opens our hearts to fully experience His grace. As we embrace the now, we affirm that God's plans for us are good, even in the midst of uncertainty.

Matthew 11:28-30 (NIV): *"Come to me, all you who are weary and burdened, and I will give you rest. Take my yoke upon you and learn from me, for I am gentle and humble in heart, and you will find rest for your souls. For my yoke is easy and my burden is light."*

This invitation reminds us that resting in God's presence allows us to release burdens and find renewal for our souls.

Living Intentionally: Thriving Through the Power of Now

Living in the present equips Christian businesswomen to approach each moment with purpose, faith, and clarity. It transforms challenges into opportunities for growth and allows us to glorify God through our actions.

Key Benefits of Embracing the Present Moment for Christian Businesswomen:

1. **Peace Through Trust**: Releasing control to God invites a deep sense of calm, as promised in Isaiah 26:3.

2. **Resilience in Challenges**: Focusing on today's opportunities strengthens our courage to face difficulties (Philippians 4:13).

3. **Joy in the Moment**: Gratitude transforms daily tasks into acts of worship, bringing joy and fulfillment (Psalm 118:24).

Conclusion: Choosing to Live Fully in God's Presence

The Power of Now is a gift for Christian businesswomen, offering a path to clarity, peace, and resilience. By living intentionally and trusting in God's provision, each moment becomes an opportunity to reflect His love, grow in faith, and glorify Him through our work and relationships.

As Matthew 5:16 (NIV) encourages:

"Let your light shine before others, that they may see your good deeds and glorify your Father in heaven."

Let us embrace the present as a sacred space where God's grace abounds, transforming ordinary moments into extraordinary opportunities to live for His glory.

Understanding God's Presence in the Current Moment

Mindfulness, when viewed through the lens of Scripture, transcends self-awareness and focuses on a profound connection with God. It involves recognizing His work in the present moment and intentionally engaging with His presence. For Christian businesswomen, this practice transforms daily challenges into opportunities to align with God's will, finding peace and clarity in His guidance.

Psalm 46:10 (NIV) offers a powerful invitation to embrace this principle:

"Be still, and know that I am God."

This verse encourages us to stop, recognize His authority, and rely on His guidance, especially in stressful or uncertain times.

Attentiveness to God's Guidance

Engaging with God in the present requires a deliberate effort to quiet the noise of life and focus on His direction. This attentiveness fosters a sense of trust, allowing His wisdom to shape decisions and actions.

Practical Example

Imagine a businesswoman preparing for a high-stakes meeting. Anxiety begins to build as she considers potential outcomes. Instead of succumbing to nervous energy, she takes a moment to pause and pray:

"Lord, guide my words and actions today. Help me reflect Your wisdom and grace."

This simple prayer shifts her focus from fear to faith, reminding her that God is with her in the moment. As she enters the meeting, she feels grounded and reassured, relying on His strength rather than her own.

Finding Calmness in Stressful Moments

Mindfulness rooted in faith allows us to experience God's peace during moments of stress. Meditating on Scriptures like Psalm 46:10

reminds us that God's sovereignty extends over every situation, no matter how overwhelming it may seem.

Practical Application

During a particularly stressful day, a woman juggling multiple responsibilities might feel the weight of her workload pressing down on her. She steps away from her desk, closes her eyes, and silently repeats the words of Psalm 46:10:

"Be still, and know that I am God."

With each repetition, she feels a sense of calm wash over her. Her perspective shifts from the chaos around her to the steadfastness of God's presence. This moment of stillness not only calms her mind but also restores her confidence to approach her tasks with clarity and purpose.

Embracing the Present as a Sacred Opportunity

Recognizing God's presence in the present moment turns ordinary moments into sacred opportunities for worship and trust. Mindful of His guidance brings peace and direction, whether in meetings, family interactions, or personal reflection.

Practical Steps for Engaging with God's Presence

1. **Start with Prayer**: Begin each day by inviting God into your plans. A simple prayer like, *"Lord, guide my steps and decisions today,"* sets a tone of reliance on Him.

2. **Pause Regularly**: Take intentional breaks throughout the day to reconnect with God, even if it's just for a minute. Reflect on verses like Proverbs 3:5-6:
   "Trust in the Lord with all your heart and lean not on your own understanding; in all your ways submit to Him, and He will make your paths straight."

3. **Focus on Gratitude**: thank God for His blessings in the

present moment. Gratitude shifts the focus from what is lacking to what is abundant.

Living with Purpose Through His Presence

By actively engaging with God's presence, Christian businesswomen can navigate their responsibilities with grace and confidence. Understanding that He is at work in the present moment allows them to trust His plan, release unnecessary worries, and embrace each day with joy and purpose.

Philippians 4:6-7 (NIV) encapsulates this beautifully:

"Do not be anxious about anything, but in every situation, by prayer and petition, with thanksgiving, present your requests to God. And the peace of God, which transcends all understanding, will guard your hearts and your minds in Christ Jesus."

When we remain attentive to God's presence in the now, we are empowered to reflect His light, tackle challenges with resilience, and find peace that only He can provide.

Practical Applications of Living in the Present

1. Intentional Pauses During the Day

When the day feels overwhelming, brief moments of stillness and prayer can reset the mind.

Example:

A businesswoman facing a conflict might take a moment to reflect on Proverbs 3:5-6 (NIV):

"Trust in the Lord with all your heart and lean not on your own understanding; in all your ways submit to Him, and He will make your paths straight."

This pause helps her respond with wisdom and grace rather than reacting impulsively.

2. Gratitude in Action

Gratitude transforms the heart by focusing on blessings rather than challenges.

How to Practice:

- Start or end the day with a gratitude list.
- Pair this practice with scriptures like James 1:17 (NIV): *"Every good and perfect gift is from above."*

For example, a woman stressed about financial pressures might thank God for opportunities and supportive colleagues, shifting her mindset from fear to faith.

3. Fully Engaging in Relationships

Being present in relationships reflects Christ's love. It involves listening attentively, offering empathy, and prioritizing people over tasks.

Example:

A leader might reflect on Ephesians 4:2 (NIV):

"Be completely humble and gentle; be patient, bearing with one another in love."

By actively listening to her team's concerns, she fosters trust and strengthens connections, creating an atmosphere of collaboration and mutual respect.

The Spiritual Power of Presence

Living in the present moment is more than a strategy for managing stress—it is a sacred act of worship and a testament to trust in God's sovereignty. It involves embracing each moment as a divine gift, an opportunity to align one's actions and thoughts with God's will. For Christian women, this mindset transforms daily routines and challenges into acts of faith and reliance on His providence.

Faith Over Fear: Trusting God in the Now

Matthew 6:34 (NIV) beautifully captures the heart of living in the present:

"Do not worry about tomorrow, for tomorrow will worry about itself. Each day has enough trouble of its own."

This teaching from Jesus encourages believers to release the weight of future uncertainties and focus instead on what God has placed before them today. Worrying about tomorrow often robs us of the peace and opportunities that exist in the present. By choosing faith over fear, Christian women can face each day with confidence, knowing that God is in control of the future.

Practical Example

A businesswoman might feel overwhelmed by an upcoming deadline or a looming financial challenge. Instead of allowing fear to take hold, she pauses to reflect on Matthew 6:34 and prays:

"Lord, help me trust in Your plan. Guide me through today's tasks and remind me that You hold tomorrow in Your hands."

This act of surrender shifts her focus from the unknown to the here and now, empowering her to approach her responsibilities with clarity and purpose.

Presence as an Act of Worship

When we intentionally live in the moment, we acknowledge God's active role in our lives. This awareness turns ordinary tasks into sacred acts of worship. Whether working, spending time with loved ones, or pausing to pray, being fully present reflects gratitude for the life God has given us.

Example of Worship in the Present

Consider a mother juggling her career and family. As she prepares dinner, instead of rushing through the task with a distracted mind, she pauses to thank God for the meal and her family. This simple act transforms a mundane chore into an expression of worship, honoring God's provision and love.

Colossians 3:23 (NIV) reinforces this mindset:

"Whatever you do, work at it with all your heart, as working for the Lord, not for human masters."

Releasing the Burden of Tomorrow

Living in the present moment allows us to release the heavy burden of future concerns. When we focus on today, we trust God to handle what lies ahead, freeing ourselves from unnecessary anxiety.

Isaiah 41:10 (NIV) offers reassurance:

"Do not fear, for I am with you; do not be dismayed, for I am your God. I will strengthen you and help you; I will uphold you with my righteous right hand."

This promise assures us that God's strength and guidance are always enough for the challenges we encounter, both now and in the future.

The Benefits of Living in the Present

1. **Deepened Trust in God**

   When we concentrate on the present, we trust in God's daily care instead of fretting about the future. Philippians 4:19 (NIV) assures us:

   "And my God will meet all your needs according to the riches of His glory in Christ Jesus."

2. **Increased Peace**

   Letting go of future concerns allows us to experience the peace of God that transcends understanding, as described in Philippians 4:7 (NIV).

3. **Purposeful Living**

   Being present helps us align our actions with God's will, turning everyday moments into opportunities to glorify Him.

Practical Steps to Embrace the Spiritual Power of Presence

1. Start Each Day with Gratitude

Begin your morning by thanking God for the gift of a new day. Reflect on Lamentations 3:22-23 (NIV):

"Because of the Lord's great love we are not consumed, for His compassions never fail. They are new every morning; great is Your faithfulness."

2. Practice Intentional Pauses

Throughout your day, take brief moments to pause, pray, and reconnect with God. Reflect on a verse like Psalm 46:10 (NIV):

"Be still, and know that I am God."

3. Focus on One Task at a Time

Avoid multitasking and focus entirely on the current task, approaching it as a sacred act.

4. Release Worries to God

When anxiety about the future arises, pray and surrender your concerns to Him. Reflect on 1 Peter 5:7 (NIV):

"Cast all your anxiety on Him because He cares for you."

Conclusion: Thriving Through God's Presence

Living in the present moment is a powerful spiritual practice that allows Christian women to fully experience God's grace, peace, and guidance. It is an act of worship that reflects trust in His sovereignty and gratitude for His blessings.

By letting go of worries about the future and embracing the present, we align ourselves with God's purpose, empowering us to approach each day with confidence and joy. As Matthew 5:16 (NIV) reminds us:

"Let your light shine before others, that they may see your good deeds and glorify your Father in heaven."

Every moment offers a chance to showcase His love, live purposefully, and glorify Him through our deeds.

Practical Techniques for Staying Present:

1. Deep Breathing

Deep breathing connects the physical and spiritual, offering a moment to pause and reset.

How to Practice:

1. **Create Space**: Find a quiet spot.

2. **Intentional Breathing**: Inhale for a count of four, hold for four, and exhale for six.

3. **Pair with Scripture**: Meditate on verses like Philippians 4:7 (NIV):
   "And the peace of God, which transcends all understanding, will guard your hearts and your minds in Christ Jesus."

Example:

During a tense meeting, pausing to take deep breaths and reflect on Psalm 46:10 can transform stress into calm trust in God's guidance.

2. Mindfulness Meditation

Mindfulness meditation integrates stillness, scripture, and prayer, grounding Christian women in God's presence.

Steps to Practice:

1. Find a quiet space free from distractions.

2. Choose a scripture, such as Matthew 6:34, to meditate on.

3. Reflect on the verse while breathing deeply.

4. Close with a prayer of gratitude or surrender.

Example:

A woman preparing for a challenging day might meditate on Isaiah 41:10 (NIV):

"Do not fear, for I am with you; do not be dismayed, for I am your God."

This practice instills courage and confidence in God's promises.

3. Mindful Walking

Mindful walking transforms routine activities into moments of worship.

How to Practice:

1. Set an intention, such as seeking God's peace.

2. Reflect on scriptures like Psalm 119:105 (NIV):
   "Your word is a lamp to my feet, a light on my path."

3. Offer prayers of gratitude as you walk.

Example:

A businesswoman on a lunch break might use a short walk to thank God for her work, reflecting on Genesis 1:31 (NIV): *"God saw all that He had made, and it was very good."*

Thriving Through Presence

Living in the present moment equips Christian women to approach life with resilience and faith. Each moment becomes an opportunity to reflect God's love and glorify Him through intentional actions.

Matthew 5:16 (NIV) encapsulates this calling:

"Let your light shine before others, that they may see your good deeds and glorify your Father in heaven."

By anchoring in God's presence, Christian businesswomen experience:

1. **Peace Through Trust**: Meditating on God's promises releases fears, fostering peace (Isaiah 26:3).
2. **Resilience in Challenges**: Trusting in Philippians 4:13 reminds women of their strength in Christ.
3. **Joy in Everyday Moments**: Gratitude transforms mundane tasks into worship.

Conclusion

For Christian businesswomen, embracing the present moment is more than mindfulness—it is a faith-filled response to God's grace. Through intentional living, gratitude practice, and focusing on God's presence, women can confidently navigate life's challenges with clarity and purpose. Every day presents a chance to honor God and mirror His love, transforming even the smallest deeds into acts of worship.

Philippians 4:7 reminds us of the reward of this intentional living: *"And the peace of God, which transcends all understanding, will guard your hearts and your minds in Christ Jesus."*

CHAPTER 5

MINDFULNESS PRACTICES FOR THE BUSY BUSINESSWOMAN

The modern businesswoman often finds herself entangled in numerous directions due to the whirlwind of deadlines, meetings, and personal commitments. For Christian women in business, the challenge is even more profound: How do you balance the demands of leadership with your desire to honor God in every aspect of your life?

The key to finding balance and peace in the midst of a busy life is mindfulness—a practice that fosters intentionality, peace, and focus in your daily routine. For Christian women, mindfulness is not just a tool for managing stress but a spiritual discipline that draws you closer to God. It's about being fully present in each moment, recognizing His hand at work in your life, and aligning your actions with His purpose.

This chapter delves into practical, faith-centered mindfulness practices aimed at empowering busy businesswomen to navigate their responsibilities with confidence and grace. From breathing techniques that calm the spirit to journaling exercises that bring clarity, these tools will empower you to stay grounded amidst the chaos, fostering emotional well-being and mental clarity. You'll learn how to integrate prayer and Scripture into everyday moments, transforming even the busiest day into an act of worship.

As Philippians 4:6-7 (NIV) reminds us:

"Do not be anxious about anything, but in every situation, by prayer and petition, with thanksgiving, present your requests to God. And the peace of God, which transcends all understanding, will guard your hearts and your minds in Christ Jesus."

Through the practices outlined in this chapter, you'll discover how to embrace this peace, cultivate resilience, and honor God in both your professional and personal life. Whether you're seeking to manage stress, foster creativity, or deepen your spiritual connection, mindfulness offers a path to balance, purpose, and fulfillment.

Exploring Breathing Techniques as a Path to Calmness and Faith

Breathing techniques serve as sacred practices for Christian businesswomen, aligning the body, mind, and spirit with God's presence beyond mere stress management tools. The simple act of focusing on one's breath can lead to profound emotional well-being, mental clarity, and spiritual renewal. When paired with prayer and Scripture, these techniques transform into powerful avenues for experiencing God's peace in the midst of life's demands.

Deep diaphragmatic breathing, also known as 'belly breathing,' involves engaging the diaphragm to promote relaxation and calmness.

Deep diaphragmatic breathing, often called "belly breathing," is a powerful method to calm the body and mind. This technique engages the diaphragm, encouraging deep inhalations through the nose and slow exhalations through the mouth. Scientifically, it activates the body's relaxation response, reducing heart rate, lowering blood pressure, and soothing the nervous system. For Christian businesswomen, this practice can also be a spiritual exercise, aligning physical calmness with faith and trust in God.

Incorporate deep diaphragmatic breathing into your daily routine by starting each morning with intentional breathing and setting aside moments for calmness before stressful situations.

1. Begin Your Workday with Intentional Breathing

Start each morning by setting aside a few minutes to breathe deeply and focus on God's presence.

- **Inhale:** Recite Psalm 46:10 (NIV): *"Be still, and know that I am God."*
- **Exhale:** Release any tension or worry, praying silently, *"Lord, I surrender this day to You."*

This practice not only calms your spirit but also readies your heart and mind, preparing you to approach the day with both purpose and peace.

2. A Moment of Calm Before Stressful Situations

Before entering a high-pressure meeting or tackling a challenging task, take a moment to practice deep breathing.

Example:

As you inhale deeply, visualize God's peace filling your body. As you exhale slowly, pray:

"Lord, fill me with Your peace and guide my words."

This simple act transforms nervous energy into trust, grounding your thoughts and enabling you to respond with clarity and confidence.

Spiritual Integration

Combining deep breathing with Scripture enhances its effectiveness, creating a meditative practice that not only calms the mind but also aligns it with God's truths, fostering a deeper spiritual connection. Reflect on Matthew 11:28-29 (NIV):

"Come to me, all you who are weary and burdened, and I will give you rest. Take my yoke upon you and learn from me, for I am gentle and humble in heart, and you will find rest for your souls."

With each breath, invite God's rest into your heart, releasing the burdens that weigh you down.

Deep diaphragmatic breathing offers physical calmness by activating the parasympathetic nervous system, mental clarity by improving focus, and spiritual alignment by creating space for connecting with God.

1. **Physical Calmness**: activates the parasympathetic nervous system, promoting relaxation.

2. **Mental Clarity**: Clears the mind, improving focus and decision-making.

3. **Spiritual Alignment**: Creates space to connect with God, transforming moments of stress into acts of worship.

Conclusion

Deep diaphragmatic breathing is more than a stress-management tool—it is a pathway to peace and a tangible reminder of God's presence in every moment. By incorporating this practice into your daily life, you invite calmness, clarity, and divine guidance, enabling you to navigate life's challenges with grace and faith.

As Isaiah 26:3 (NIV) promises:

"You will keep in perfect peace those whose minds are steadfast because they trust in you."

Trust in God, breathe deeply, and let His peace guard your heart and mind.

Embracing Mindful Prayer Through the 4-7-8 Breathing Technique

Dr. Andrew Weil's 4-7-8 breathing technique is a method for calming the body and mind that has solid scientific support. It engages the parasympathetic nervous system, reducing stress and promoting relaxation (Weil, 2011). For Christian businesswomen, integrating this technique with prayer and Scripture creates a meaningful spiritual practice that deepens trust in God while managing stress effectively.

How to Practice the 4-7-8 Technique

1. **Inhale for 4 Counts.**

   As you breathe in deeply, recite silently:

   "Lord, You are my strength."

   This affirmation is rooted in Psalm 28:7 (NIV):

   "The Lord is my strength and my shield; my heart trusts in Him, and He helps me."

2. **Hold for 7 Counts**

   During the pause, meditate on Isaiah 41:10 (NIV):

   "Do not fear, for I am with you; do not be dismayed, for I am your God. I will strengthen you and help you; I will uphold you with my righteous right hand."

   Reflecting on this verse fosters reassurance and confidence in God's unwavering presence.

3. **Exhale for 8 Counts**

As you release the breath slowly, whisper:
"I trust in Your plan."
This act of surrender aligns with Proverbs 3:5-6 (NIV):
"Trust in the Lord with all your heart and lean not on your own understanding; in all your ways submit to Him, and He will make your paths straight."

Practical Applications of the 4-7-8 Technique

1. Before Stressful Situations

Research shows that controlled breathing lowers cortisol levels, improving emotional regulation (Sinha et al., 2011). Use this method to calm your mind and spirit before challenging moments.

Example:

Before entering a high-pressure meeting, practice the 4-7-8 technique, focusing on Isaiah 41:10. The act of breathing deeply paired with Scripture shifts your mindset from anxiety to trust in God's strength.

2. During Overwhelming Moments

Studies indicate that breathing exercises can significantly reduce feelings of overwhelm by decreasing the body's fight-or-flight response (Brown et al., 2005).

Example:

In the middle of a busy day, pause to practice this technique. Visualize handing your worries to God as you exhale, allowing His peace to fill your heart, as promised in Philippians 4:6-7 (NIV).

3. At the End of the Day

Practicing the 4-7-8 technique at night can improve sleep quality, as it reduces heart rate and promotes relaxation (National Sleep Foundation, 2020).

Example:

Reflect on Psalm 4:8 (NIV):

"In peace I will lie down and sleep, for You alone, Lord, make me dwell in safety."

Combine this verse with your breath as you release the day's burdens and prepare yourself for restful sleep.

The Spiritual Impact of 4-7-8 Breathing

Pairing breathing techniques with Scripture transforms them into acts of worship and trust. Philippians 4:6-7 (NIV) underscores the peace that comes through prayerful surrender:

"Do not be anxious about anything, but in every situation, by prayer and petition, with thanksgiving, present your requests to God. And the peace of God, which transcends all understanding, will guard your hearts and your minds in Christ Jesus."

Aligning your breath with prayer creates a sacred rhythm that intertwines your physical well-being with your spiritual faith, fostering a deep connection with God.

Conclusion

The 4-7-8 breathing technique is more than a relaxation method—it is an invitation to connect with God and experience His peace. Through the integration of Scripture and prayer into this practice, Christian businesswomen can effectively manage stress while strengthening their reliance on God's guidance.

Breath-Focused Meditation: Centering on God's Word

Breath-focused meditation combines intentional breathing with the truths of Scripture, offering Christian women a way to pause, reflect, and reconnect with God's promises. This practice not only calms the mind but also serves as an act of worship, deepening one's spiritual connection and fostering peace in the midst of life's demands.

The Power of Breath and Scripture

When paired with God's Word, the act of mindful breathing becomes a sacred rhythm that aligns the physical and spiritual. Philippians 4:6-7 (NIV) beautifully encapsulates this practice:

"Do not be anxious about anything, but in every situation, by prayer and petition, with thanksgiving, present your requests to God. And the peace of God, which transcends all understanding, will guard your hearts and your minds in Christ Jesus."

By meditating on verses like this, each breath becomes a prayer, and each exhalation a release of worry into God's capable hands.

How to Practice Breath-Focused Meditation

1. Find a Quiet Space

Choose a location free from distractions. This could be a corner of your office, your car before a meeting, or your favorite chair at home.

2. Focus on Your Breath

Begin with slow, deep breaths. Inhale deeply through your nose, allowing your belly to rise, and exhale slowly through your mouth. Let your breathing set a steady rhythm.

3. Meditate on Scripture

Select a verse that resonates with your current season. For instance:

- **Philippians 4:6-7**: When feeling anxious, focus on the promise of God's peace.

- **Psalm 46:10 (NIV)**: *"Be still, and know that I am God."* Use this verse to anchor your thoughts during moments of uncertainty.

As you inhale, silently recite part of the verse (*"Be still"*). As you exhale, complete it (*"and know that I am God"*). Repeat this process, allowing the words to settle deeply in your heart.

4. Align Your Breath with the Verse

Let the rhythm of your breathing match the cadence of the verse. For example:

- Inhale deeply, focusing on the phrase, *"Do not be anxious."*
- Exhale slowly, reflecting on, *"The peace of God will guard your heart."*

Practical Applications

Start Your Day with Clarity

Use breath-focused meditation in the morning to center your thoughts and dedicate your day to God. Reflect on Lamentations 3:22-23 (NIV):

"Because of the Lord's great love we are not consumed, for His compassions never fail. They are new every morning; great is Your faithfulness."

Midday Recalibration

Pause during a busy afternoon to refocus. Meditate on Isaiah 26:3 (NIV):

"You will keep in perfect peace those whose minds are steadfast, because they trust in You."

This practice can help you regain calmness and clarity.

Evening Reflection

End your day by meditating on Psalm 4:8 (NIV):

"In peace I will lie down and sleep, for You alone, Lord, make me dwell in safety."

This can provide closure and prepare your mind for restful sleep.

The Benefits of Breath-Focused Meditation

Breath-focused meditation not only reduces stress and enhances spiritual growth but also fosters mental clarity and aligns thoughts with God's promises.

1. **Stress Reduction**: Slowing the breath calms the nervous

system, reducing cortisol levels and fostering relaxation (Sinha et al., 2011).

2. **Spiritual Growth**: Meditating on Scripture deepens your relationship with God and aligns your thoughts with His promises.

3. **Mental Clarity**: Pausing to breathe and reflect enhances focus and decision-making.

A Sacred Reminder of God's Presence

Breath-focused meditation elevates a simple act into a sacred connection with God, deepening one's spiritual bond and fostering a sense of divine presence. It reminds us that His presence is accessible in every moment, providing peace and guidance amidst life's chaos.

As Psalm 19:14 (NIV) declares:

"May these words of my mouth and this meditation of my heart be pleasing in your sight, Lord, my Rock and my Redeemer."

Incorporating this practice into your daily routine establishes a rhythm of mindfulness and worship that empowers you to gracefully navigate challenges with unwavering trust and grace. Each breath becomes a testimony to God's faithfulness, renewing your spirit and grounding your heart in His unfailing love.

Consistency in incorporating breathing techniques into your daily routine is key to experiencing lasting peace and strengthening your connection with God.

Like physical exercise, breathing techniques benefit from regular practice. Establishing a routine that includes intentional breathing—whether in the morning, during work breaks, or before bed—builds resilience and fosters a deeper reliance on God.

Example:

End each day with deep breathing paired with Psalm 4:8 (NIV):

"In peace I will lie down and sleep, for You alone, Lord, make me dwell in safety."

This practice not only calms the mind but also prepares the spirit for restful sleep.

Incorporating biblical themes into guided meditations, such as focusing on verses like Philippians 4:6-7, can deepen the spiritual experience and lead to reflections on God's peace.

Guided meditations offer a structured approach to mindfulness, helping Christian businesswomen connect with God, reduce stress, and center their thoughts. These intentional pauses create sacred spaces in the midst of busy schedules, fostering emotional balance and spiritual growth.

Biblical Themes in Guided Meditations

Incorporating Scripture into meditations enhances their spiritual depth. For instance, a session might begin with Philippians 4:6-7, leading participants to reflect on God's peace.

Example of Guided Meditation:

1. **Start with a Verse:** Begin by reading Matthew 11:28-29 (NIV):
   "Come to me, all you who are weary and burdened, and I will give you rest. Take my yoke upon you and learn from me, for I am gentle and humble in heart, and you will find rest for your souls."

2. **Visualization:** Imagine placing your burdens at Jesus' feet and receiving His peace.

3. **Prayer:** Conclude with a prayer of gratitude, thanking God for His presence.

This practice transforms meditation into an act of worship, strengthening faith and promoting calmness.

Visualization for Christian Ambitions

Guided meditations can include visualizing professional and personal goals within a framework of faith. Imagine your business thriving under God's guidance, aligning your actions with His purpose. Proverbs 16:3 (NIV) encourages this approach:

"Commit to the Lord whatever you do, and He will establish your plans."

Practical Example:

During meditation, envision your work contributing to God's kingdom—whether through ethical leadership, community impact, or acts of kindness.

The Benefits of Breath-Focused Meditation

Journaling as an act of worship allows Christian women to process thoughts, reflect on God's guidance, and deepen their faith, transforming the act of writing into a sacred practice of aligning actions with God's purpose.

Journaling is more than a productivity tool—it is a spiritual discipline that allows Christian businesswomen to process thoughts, reflect on God's guidance, and deepen their faith. It transforms the act of writing into worship, creating space to align one's actions with God's purpose. Research highlights journaling as an effective way to reduce stress and gain clarity (Smyth et al., 2018). When paired with prayer and Scripture, it becomes a powerful way to connect with God.

The Power of Journaling for Christian Women

Journaling allows women to step back from the chaos of daily life and intentionally focus on God's presence and promises. It creates a tangible record of spiritual growth and helps cultivate gratitude and resilience.

Habakkuk 2:2 (NIV) underscores the importance of recording revelations:

"Write down the revelation and make it plain on tablets so that a herald may run with it."

By documenting prayers, reflections, and challenges, journaling becomes a way to preserve God's guidance for future encouragement and testimony.

Types of Journaling Practices

1. Prayer Journals

A prayer journal is a space to document conversations with God. Writing prayers encourages intentionality and allows you to see how God answers them over time. Research shows that journaling fosters mindfulness, which enhances emotional well-being and spiritual growth (Pennebaker, 1997).

How to Use a Prayer Journal:

- Write specific requests and concerns.
- Document answered prayers to build faith during difficult seasons.
- Reflect on the ways in which God is actively working in your life.

Example Entry: "Lord, *help me be clear as I lead my team today. May my actions and decisions reflect Your grace. Thank You for Your guidance and provision."*

Scriptural Anchor:

Psalm 34:4 (NIV):

"I sought the Lord, and He answered me; He delivered me from all my fears."

2. Gratitude Journals

Gratitude journaling focuses on recognizing and appreciating God's blessings. Studies reveal that practicing gratitude increases emotional resilience and reduces stress (Emmons & McCullough, 2003).

How to Practice Gratitude Journaling:

- Write three things you are grateful for each day.
- Pair your entries with verses of thankfulness.

Example Entry: *"Thank You, Lord, for the strength to face today, the encouragement from my team, and the beauty of the sunset that reminds me of Your faithfulness."*

Scriptural Anchor:

James 1:17 (NIV):

"Every good and perfect gift is from above, coming down from the Father of the heavenly lights, who does not change like shifting shadows."

3. Problem-Solving Through Writing

When faced with challenges, journaling helps process emotions and explore potential solutions. Writing provides clarity and allows you to seek God's wisdom in decision-making.

How to Approach Problem-Solving Journaling:

1. Write down the challenge in detail.
2. List possible solutions.
3. Pray for guidance and reflect on relevant Scriptures.

Example Entry: *"Lord, I'm struggling to balance work and family. Show me how to prioritize according to Your will. I trust in Your promise to guide my path."*

Scriptural Guidance:

Proverbs 3:5-6 (NIV):

"Trust in the Lord with all your heart and lean not on your own understanding; in all your ways submit to Him, and He will make your paths straight."

The Benefits of Journaling

1. Spiritual Growth

Journaling creates space for reflection, allowing you to deepen your relationship with God and align your actions with His purpose.

2. Stress Reduction

Research confirms that journaling reduces stress by providing an outlet for processing emotions (Smyth et al., 2018).

3. Gratitude and Perspective

Focusing on blessings through gratitude journaling fosters a positive outlook and strengthens faith.

4. Self-Discovery and Clarity

Journaling enhances self-awareness, helping you identify patterns and make thoughtful decisions.

Making Journaling a Daily Habit

Consistency is vital for making journaling impactful. Start small, dedicating five to ten minutes each day to write and rereflecting

Tips for Successful Journaling:

- **Set Aside Time**: Morning or evening works well for reflection and prayer.

- **Be Honest**: Write openly about your struggles and victories.

- **Incorporate Scripture**: Let God's Word guide your journaling.

- **Revisit Entries**: Reflect on past entries to see God's faithfulness over time.

Conclusion: Writing as Worship

Journaling goes beyond mental exercise; it is a spiritual practice that invites God into every aspect of one's daily life, fostering a profound connection and alignment with His will. It provides clarity, strengthens faith, and creates a lasting record of God's work in one's life.

Psalm 119:105 (NIV) reminds us:

"Your word is a lamp to my feet, a light on my path."

Through committing time to journaling, Christian businesswomen can gracefully navigate challenges, nurture their faith, and radiate God's light in all aspects of life.

Conclusion: Integrating Faith and Mindfulness

Breathing techniques, guided meditations, and journaling go beyond stress-management tools; they are spiritual practices that enrich one's relationship with God. By integrating these disciplines into daily routines, Christian businesswomen can confidently navigate life's challenges with peace, clarity, and resilience.

Philippians 4:13 (NIV) reminds us of the strength we gain through Christ:

"I can do all this through Him who gives me strength."

Through these practices, women can undergo profound transformation, live purposefully, and radiate God's grace in every facet of their lives.

CHAPTER 6

UNDERSTANDING GRATITUDE FROM A CHRISTIAN PERSPECTIVE

Gratitude goes beyond feeling thankful for blessings; it is a deep spiritual practice that changes our lives and connects us with God's plans. In a Christian context, gratitude signifies a deep trust in God's sovereignty, a profound recognition of His abundant blessings, and a sincere acknowledgment of His unwavering goodness, irrespective of circumstances. It's a consistent theme throughout Scripture, urging believers to cultivate a heart of gratitude intentionally as a fundamental aspect of worship and faith.

1 Thessalonians 5:16-18 (NIV) serves as a cornerstone for this principle:

"Rejoice always, pray continually, and give thanks in all circumstances; for this is God's will for you in Christ Jesus."

This passage emphasizes the need for lasting gratitude, not just a momentary response, to influence every part of life. For Christian businesswomen, gratitude becomes a tool for navigating challenges with resilience, enhancing relationships, and fostering a mindset of abundance and peace.

Gratitude is not just an emotional response; it is a spiritual discipline woven into the Bible. From Genesis to Revelation, Scripture calls God's people to recognize and give thanks for His provision, grace, and sovereignty. Gratitude shows a heart in tune with God's plans, leading to a closer bond with Him and a fresh outlook on life.

The Bible often ties gratitude to worship, highlighting its importance in acknowledging God's greatness. **Psalm 100:4** (NIV) reminds us to:

"Enter His gates with thanksgiving and His courts with praise; give thanks to Him and praise His name."

This verse emphasizes that thanksgiving is an integral part of approaching God. It invites believers to come before Him with a heart full of gratitude, recognizing His blessings and sovereignty.

In the Old Testament, gratitude found institutional expression in practices like the Feast of Weeks and the Feast of Tabernacles, where communal celebrations were held to express gratitude for God's provision and faithfulness. These celebrations were designed to thank God for His provision and to remind the Israelites of His faithfulness **(Deuteronomy 16:10–11).** Such communal acts of gratitude fostered a culture that revered God and acknowledged His role in their lives.

Example:

Imagine a farmer during biblical times standing in his field during the harvest season, lifting a sheaf of grain as an offering to God in gratitude for the bountiful yield. This act symbolized not only thankfulness for material provision but also trust in God for future needs.

Paul's Teachings on Gratitude in the New Testament

The New Testament expands the concept of gratitude, urging believers to practice thankfulness in every circumstance. **Philippians 4:6-7** (NIV) underscores the transformative power of gratitude in prayer:

"Do not be anxious about anything, but in every situation, by prayer and petition, with thanksgiving, present your requests to God. And the peace of God, which transcends all understanding, will guard your hearts and your minds in Christ Jesus."

Here, Paul highlights that gratitude shifts our focus from worries to God's faithfulness. By giving thanks, even amid trials, believers experience divine peace that surpasses human comprehension.

Example:

Consider a Christian businesswoman facing a significant financial setback. Instead of succumbing to anxiety, she pauses to thank God for the wisdom He has given her in the past, trusting that He will guide her through this challenge. This act of faith transforms her perspective, enabling her to approach the situation with calmness and clarity.

Paul also emphasizes gratitude as a defining characteristic of the Christian life. In **Colossians 3:15-17** (NIV), he writes:

"Let the peace of Christ rule in your hearts, since as members of one body you were called to peace. And be thankful. Let the message of Christ dwell among you richly as you teach and admonish one another with all wisdom..... And whatever you do, whether in word or deed, do it all in the name of the Lord Jesus, giving thanks to God the Father through Him."

This passage underscores that gratitude should permeate every aspect of life, from individual actions to community worship.

Gratitude in the Face of Trials

Biblical gratitude is not confined to seasons of abundance; its true potency shines through in the midst of adversity and trials. The Bible repeatedly calls believers to give thanks, even when circumstances are challenging. This practice reflects trust in God's sovereignty and faithfulness.

1 Thessalonians 5:16-18 (NIV) captures this principle succinctly:
"Rejoice always, pray continually, and give thanks in all circumstances; for this is God's will for you in Christ Jesus."

Example:
A widow who has lost her spouse might find solace in thanking God for the years they shared together. As she prays, she begins to experience healing and hope, trusting that God will continue to provide comfort and guidance in the days ahead.

Even Jesus modeled gratitude in the face of hardship. Before feeding the 5,000, He gave thanks for the meager five loaves and two fish, trusting God to multiply them (**John 6:11**). This act of gratitude preceded a miraculous provision, reminding us of the power of thankfulness in unlocking divine blessings.

Gratitude as an Act of Faith

Gratitude is the ultimate expression of faith. It recognizes that every good gift originates from God (James 1:17) and demonstrates a steadfast trust in His immutable nature. Even when life feels uncertain, gratitude grounds us in the assurance of God's presence and provision.

Example:
A Christian entrepreneur navigating a challenging season in her business reflects on **Psalm 107:1** (NIV):
"Give thanks to the Lord, for He is good; His love endures forever."
This verse reminds her that God's goodness is constant, empowering her to face difficulties with renewed courage and hope.

Practical Steps to Cultivate Biblical Gratitude

1. **Start Each Day with Thanksgiving:**

Begin your morning by thanking God for specific blessings. Pair this practice with a verse like **Psalm 118:24** (NIV): "This is the day the Lord has made; let us rejoice and be glad in it."

2. **Incorporate Gratitude into Prayer:**
   Dedicate part of your prayer time to listing things you're grateful for, even the small joys.

3. **Practice Gratitude Journaling:**
   Write down three things you are thankful for each evening, reflecting on how God was present in your day.

4. **Share Gratitude with Others:**
   Express appreciation to friends, family, and colleagues. A simple "thank you" can brighten someone's day and foster a culture of gratitude.

5. **Meditate on Scripture:**
   Memorize and meditate on gratitude-focused verses, such as **Colossians 4:2** (NIV):
   "Devote yourselves to prayer, being watchful and thankful."

Conclusion: Living a Life of Gratitude

Gratitude stands as a potent spiritual discipline that not only reshapes our hearts but also enriches our faith, forging a deeper connection with God. By embracing thankfulness in every circumstance, we reflect His goodness and demonstrate our trust in His plans.

Final Reflection:

Let gratitude become the lens through which you view your life. As you cultivate a thankful heart, you will discover a renewed sense of joy, peace, and purpose, empowering you to navigate life's challenges with grace and confidence.

The Transformative Power of Gratitude

1. Gratitude as a Stress Reliever

Practicing gratitude has been shown to significantly reduce stress and improve mental health. Research published in the *Journal of Positive Psychology* found that individuals who regularly expressed gratitude experienced greater emotional well-being and resilience (Emmons & McCullough, 2003).

For Christian businesswomen, this means intentionally shifting their focus from challenges to blessings and trusting in God's provision even in difficult seasons.

Example: During a challenging financial quarter, a business leader reflects on how God has provided in the past, thanking Him for the wisdom to navigate the current situation.

Scriptural Anchor: Psalm 46:1 (NIV):
"God is our refuge and strength, an ever-present help in trouble."

2. Gratitude and Relationships

Gratitude fosters stronger connections by encouraging appreciation and mutual respect. Expressing thanks to colleagues, clients, and family members creates a culture of positivity and collaboration.

Example: A Christian entrepreneur takes time during a team meeting to thank employees for their dedication, aligning this practice with the principle of honoring others as outlined in **Romans 12:10** (NIV):
"Be devoted to one another in love. Honor one another above yourselves."

3. Gratitude as a Faith-Strengthening Practice

Gratitude deepens faith by shifting focus from personal abilities to God's sovereignty. Recognizing His hand in every detail of life fosters trust and humility.

Example: Reflecting on past challenges that led to unexpected blessings helps a businesswoman trust God's plan in her current struggles.

Scriptural Anchor: James 1:17 (NIV):
"Every good and perfect gift is from above, coming down from the Father of the heavenly lights, who does not change like shifting shadows."

Daily Practices to Cultivate Gratitude

1. Start a Gratitude Journal

Writing down blessings each day reinforces a positive mindset. Research shows that journaling about gratitude can increase happiness by 10% (Seligman et al., 2005).

Example: Each morning, write three things you're thankful for, pairing them with a verse like **Lamentations 3:22-23** (NIV):
"Because of the Lord's great love, we are not consumed, for His compassions never fail. They are new every morning; great is Your faithfulness."

2. Incorporate Gratitude into Prayer

Begin and end prayers with thanksgiving, acknowledging God's blessings and His presence in your life.

Example:
Morning prayer: "Lord, thank You for the opportunities You've given me today. Guide my steps to honor You."

Evening prayer: "Thank You, Father, for the strength to complete my tasks and for the blessings I encountered."

Scriptural Anchor:Colossians 4:2 (NIV):
"Devote yourselves to prayer, being watchful and thankful."

3. Practice Mindful Gratitude

Take moments throughout the day to pause, breathe deeply, and reflect on God's goodness in the present moment.

Example: While enjoying a quiet lunch, silently thank God for the nourishment and the time to recharge.

Scriptural Anchor: Psalm 34:8 (NIV):
"Taste and see that the Lord is good; blessed is the one who takes refuge in Him."

4. Share Gratitude with Others

Expressing appreciation builds relationships and fosters a culture of encouragement.

Example: Send a handwritten thank-you note to a mentor or colleague, acknowledging their impact on your life.

Scriptural Anchor: Hebrews 10:24-25 (NIV):
"And let us consider how we may spur one another on toward love and good deeds, not giving up meeting together.... but encouraging one another."

Transforming Challenges into Blessings

Despite their often daunting nature, challenges hold the potential for transformation and opportunity. For Christian businesswomen, adopting a mindset of gratitude and faith can help them reframe obstacles as stepping stones to growth and deeper reliance on God. By trusting in His purpose, even the most difficult situations can reveal unexpected blessings.

The Perspective of Faith in Challenges

The Bible promises that God can turn any challenge into something good. **Romans 8:28** (NIV) reminds us:
"And we know that in all things God works for the good of those who love Him, who have been called according to His purpose."

This promise offers reassurance that every difficulty, no matter how insurmountable, serves a greater purpose. Challenges test and refine us, shaping our character and deepening our trust in God.

Example:

A businesswoman who suddenly loses a major client might initially feel discouraged and uncertain about her future. However, as she leans into prayer and reflection, she recalls past instances when God turned setbacks into breakthroughs. This faith allows her to reframe the situation, opening her heart to new opportunities and creative solutions.

Gratitude in Adversity

Cultivating gratitude during challenges shifts the focus from loss to possibility. Gratitude recognizes God's control and welcomes His peace during hard situations.

Practical Steps:

1. **Pause and Reflect:** Take a moment to assess the situation through the lens of faith. Ask, "What might God be teaching me through this?"

2. **Pray with Thanksgiving:** Follow the guidance of **Philippians 4:6-7** (NIV):
   "Do not be anxious about anything, but in every situation, by prayer and petition, with thanksgiving, present your requests to God. And the peace of God, which transcends all understanding, will guard your hearts and your minds in Christ Jesus."
   Expressing thanks even in adversity shifts the mindset toward trust and hope.

3. **Journal the Journey:** Documenting your challenges and the blessings that emerge can provide clarity and reveal pat-

terns of God's faithfulness over time.

Turning Setbacks into Opportunities

Many challenges force us to step outside of our comfort zones, leading to growth and new perspectives. A closed door may redirect us to a path that better aligns with God's purpose for our lives.

Scriptural Inspiration:

Proverbs 3:5-6 (NIV) encourages:
"Trust in the Lord with all your heart and lean not on your own understanding; in all your ways submit to Him, and He will make your paths straight."

Example:

A woman loses her position at a company due to restructuring. While initially disheartened, she uses the time to develop a skill she had long overlooked. This new expertise leads her to a better job opportunity where her talents are more appreciated, and she feels a stronger sense of purpose.

The Role of Community in Challenges

Fellowship provides support and encouragement during trials. Sharing struggles with a trusted community allows others to offer prayer, wisdom, and practical assistance.

Hebrews 10:24-25 (NIV) underscores this importance:
"And let us consider how we may spur one another on toward love and good deeds, not giving up meeting together... but encouraging one another."

Example:

A Christian entrepreneur struggling to maintain her business during an economic downturn seeks counsel from her church's business-women's group. Their prayers and advice not only uplift her spirit but also provide actionable insights that help her navigate the challenges successfully.

God's Provision in the Midst of Challenges

The ultimate blessing in challenges is experiencing God's provision and presence. Trusting in Him through trials reveals His faithfulness and strengthens our relationship with Him.

Isaiah 41:10 (NIV) offers comfort:

"So do not fear, for I am with you; do not be dismayed, for I am your God. I will strengthen you and help you; I will uphold you with my righteous right hand."

Example:

A businesswoman facing financial struggles turns to God in prayer. In a moment of surrender, she experiences peace and receives unexpected support from a client who refers her to a lucrative opportunity.

The Ripple Effect of Overcoming Challenges

Our testimonies inspire others as we transform challenges into blessings. Sharing stories of strength and faith can motivate others in similar situations, showing that God is always faithful.

Psalm 107:2 (NIV):

"Let the redeemed of the Lord tell their story—those He redeemed from the hand of the foe."

Example:

After overcoming significant obstacles in launching her business, a woman speaks at a local conference, sharing how faith and gratitude sustained her. Her testimony inspires attendees to persevere in their own journeys.

Embracing Challenges with Gratitude

Challenges are inevitable, but their outcomes depend on how we approach them. When we choose gratitude, trust, and faith, we allow

God to work through our circumstances, turning setbacks into opportunities for growth and blessings.

Final Reflection:

James 1:2-4 (NIV) encourages:

"Consider it pure joy, my brothers and sisters, whenever you face trials of many kinds, because you know that the testing of your faith produces perseverance. Let perseverance finish its work so that you may be mature and complete, not lacking anything."

By embracing this perspective, Christian businesswomen can face challenges with courage and grace, knowing that God is always at work, transforming difficulties into blessings that strengthen their faith and fulfill His purpose.

Conclusion: Living a Life of Gratitude

Gratitude is more than just a feeling; it's a deliberate decision to see God's influence in all parts of our lives. It is a spiritual discipline that transforms the way we view challenges, approach work, and nurture our relationships. For Christian businesswomen, gratitude serves as a wellspring of resilience, a pathway to deeper faith, and a beacon that illuminates and inspires those around them.

Gratitude as a Daily Discipline

Incorporating gratitude into daily routines allows us to live with greater peace and purpose. Whether through morning prayers of thanksgiving, journaling blessings, or pausing to reflect during a busy day, these practices ground us in God's truth and remind us of His constant provision.

Example:

A woman starting her day may begin with a simple prayer:

"Lord, thank You for this new day, for the opportunities it holds, and for Your presence in every moment."

This mindset shapes her interactions and decisions, filling her workday with intention and joy.

Scriptural Anchor:

1 Thessalonians 5:16-18 (NIV):

"Rejoice always, pray continually, give thanks in all circumstances; for this is God's will for you in Christ Jesus."

Gratitude in Challenges

Gratitude shifts our perspective, especially during trials. Choosing to thank God amid difficulties demonstrates trust in His sovereignty and opens our eyes to hidden blessings. Challenges improve us, build our faith, and prepare us for bigger chances.

Example:

A businesswoman facing a major setback chooses to reflect on past challenges where God provided solutions and strength. This act of gratitude renews her hope and equips her to navigate current difficulties with resilience.

Reflection Verse:

James 1:2-4 (NIV):

"Consider it pure joy, my brothers and sisters, whenever you face trials of many kinds, because you know that the testing of your faith produces perseverance."

Gratitude in Relationships

Living with gratitude strengthens relationships, both personally and professionally. Expressing appreciation to colleagues, employees, friends, and family fosters trust and collaboration. Gratitude builds a culture of positivity, where individuals feel valued and supported.

Practical Tip:

Write a thank-you note to a colleague or take a moment to verbally express appreciation for someone's efforts.

Biblical Wisdom:

Colossians 3:15 (NIV):

"Let the peace of Christ rule in your hearts, since as members of one body you were called to peace. And be thankful."

Gratitude as a Testament of Faith

Living gratefully shows how good God is. When we choose thankfulness, we reflect His light and inspire others to recognize His faithfulness in their own lives. Our gratitude becomes a powerful tool for ministry, demonstrating the joy and peace found in Christ.

Example:

A Christian businesswoman shares her gratitude journey at a networking event, emphasizing how faith has guided her through challenges. Her story encourages others to seek God's presence in their own professional and personal lives.

Call to Action:

Psalm 107:1 (NIV):

"Give thanks to the Lord, for He is good; His love endures forever."

Final Reflection: A Grateful Life

Gratitude acts as a lens through which we perceive God's presence in every moment, whether amidst abundant blessings or the refining fires of challenges. Embracing gratitude helps us follow God's plan and leads to a life filled with peace, joy, and purpose.

Psalm 118:24 (NIV):

"This is the day the Lord has made; let us rejoice and be glad in it."

Let gratitude be the melody of your heart, shaping your words, guiding your actions, and inspiring those around you. In all situations, let us embody women of faith who not only acknowledge the limitless grace of God but also respond with unwavering thankfulness. Through this, we glorify Him and embody His love in our lives, work, and communities.

CHAPTER 7

SETTING BOUNDARIES FOR BETTER BALANCE

In today's fast-paced world, setting boundaries is more than just a helpful tool—it is a crucial component of mental, emotional, and spiritual well-being. For Christian businesswomen, this practice aligns with biblical principles of stewardship, rest, and prioritization. Boundaries allow women to focus on God's calling, manage stress effectively, and maintain a sense of balance amid competing demands. As Proverbs 4:23 (NIV) reminds us:

"Above all else, guard your heart, for everything you do flows from it."

This chapter explores the importance of identifying stress triggers, learning to say no, and prioritizing self-care as integral steps toward achieving balance and living a life that honors God.

Identifying Stress Triggers

Recognizing and addressing stress triggers is a foundational step in managing them effectively. Stress triggers are specific situations, events, or stimuli that provoke feelings of anxiety, overwhelm, or frustration. By identifying these triggers, Christian businesswomen can develop strategies to mitigate their impact, align their responses with biblical principles, and enhance their well-being. This self-awareness reflects the biblical call for self-examination and mindfulness, as seen in Psalm 139:23-24 (NIV):

"Search me, God, and know my heart; test me and know my anxious thoughts. See if there is any offensive way in me, and lead me in the way everlasting."

Identifying stress triggers invites us to partner with God in examining our hearts and lives, acknowledging the challenges we face, and seeking His guidance for peace and resilience.

1. Common Stress Triggers for Christian Businesswomen

Time pressure, resulting from juggling work deadlines, family responsibilities, and personal commitments, can make Christian businesswomen feel pressured and inadequate.

Time pressure is a pervasive stressor for many women. The demands of balancing work deadlines, family obligations, and personal commitments can lead to feelings of urgency and inadequacy. When schedules become overloaded, the resulting strain often leads to chronic stress and exhaustion.

Practical Solution:

To counteract time pressure, it's essential to prioritize moments of stillness and intentionality throughout the day. Incorporate focused breathing exercises, brief prayers, or moments of reflection.

Morning Practice

Begin your day with quiet time, reflecting on Psalm 90:12 (NIV):

"Teach us to number our days, that we may gain a heart of wisdom."

Additional Tip:

Break tasks into manageable steps and dedicate time blocks for focused work. As you plan your day, commit it to God's care, drawing strength from Proverbs 16:3 (NIV):

"Commit to the Lord whatever you do, and He will establish your plans."

Interpersonal Conflict

Conflict in relationships with colleagues, clients, or even family members is a significant stressor. Miscommunication, differing values, or unresolved tensions can amplify feelings of frustration or anxiety. However, addressing conflicts with empathy, grace, and prayer can lead to understanding and reconciliation.

Example:

Imagine a situation where a colleague misunderstands your input during a meeting. Instead of reacting defensively, pause to pray:

"Lord, grant me patience and wisdom to respond with grace."

During the conversation, reflect on Ephesians 4:2-3 (NIV):

"Be completely humble and gentle; be patient, bearing with one another in love. Make every effort to keep the unity of the Spirit through the bond of peace."

Practice active listening and seek to understand the other person's perspective before responding. Addressing conflict calmly not only alleviates stress but also models Christ-like humility and love.

Environmental Factors

Our surroundings significantly impact our mood and productivity. A cluttered workspace, excessive noise, or insufficient natural light can contribute to stress and reduce efficiency. By cultivating an organized, peaceful environment, you create a space that supports focus and calmness.

- Declutter your workspace by organizing materials and removing unnecessary items.
- Add elements of nature, such as plants or flowers, to create a soothing atmosphere.

- Use calming colors and soft lighting to foster a sense of tranquility.

Scriptural Anchor:

Reflect on 1 Corinthians 14:33 (NIV):

"For God is not a God of disorder but of peace."

Example:

A businesswoman rearranges her desk, ensuring a clear workspace and adding a small plant. She places a framed scripture verse, such as Isaiah 26:3 (NIV):

"You will keep in perfect peace those whose minds are steadfast because they trust in you."

Perfectionism

Perfectionism, a subtle stress factor, frequently causes Christian businesswomen to feel inadequate and burned out, impeding their alignment with God's purpose. Many women place immense pressure on themselves to achieve flawless results in every aspect of their lives. This unrealistic standard can rob them of joy and peace.

Reflection:

The Bible reminds us that God's grace is sufficient, and His power is made perfect in our weaknesses. Meditate on 2 Corinthians 12:9 (NIV):

"My grace is sufficient for you, for my power is made perfect in weakness."

Practical Solution:

Adopt a mindset of progress over perfection. Celebrate small victories and acknowledge your efforts without focusing solely on outcomes.

Example:

Instead of striving for an unattainable standard in a work project, a woman sets realistic goals and reflects on how God equips her for success. She prays:

"Lord, thank You for the talents You've given me. Help me to trust in Your plan and embrace progress over perfection."

2. Strategies for Identifying and Addressing Stress Triggers

1. **Practice Daily Reflection:**
   Set aside time each evening to journal about the day's challenges and moments of stress. Ask yourself:

   - What situations triggered feelings of anxiety or overwhelm?
   - How did I respond, and what could I do differently next time?

Pair this reflection with Psalm 139:23-24, inviting God to reveal areas for growth and peace.

1. **Track Patterns:**
   Keep a stress journal to identify recurring triggers. Over time, patterns will emerge, helping you develop targeted strategies to address these issues.

2. **Incorporate Prayer:**
   Begin your day by surrendering your schedule to God, asking for guidance and strength to navigate stressors. Reflect on Philippians 4:6-7 (NIV):
   "Do not be anxious about anything, but in every situation, by prayer and petition, with thanksgiving, present your requests to God. And the peace of God, which transcends all understanding, will guard your hearts and your minds in Christ Jesus."

3. **Seek Support:**
   Share your stress triggers with a trusted friend, mentor, or

small group. Their insights and encouragement can provide fresh perspectives and practical advice.

Conclusion: Aligning Responses with God's Peace

Identifying stress triggers is not just a practical exercise—it is an act of faith and mindfulness. By recognizing the specific factors that challenge your peace, you invite God into those moments, trusting Him to guide and strengthen you.

As you navigate the complexities of life and work, remember the promise of Isaiah 41:10 (NIV):

"So do not fear, for I am with you; do not be dismayed, for I am your God. I will strengthen you and help you; I will uphold you with my righteous right hand."

Through prayer, intentional reflection, and proactive strategies, you can transform stress triggers into opportunities for growth and reliance on God's grace. Let each challenge draw you closer to Him, fostering peace, clarity, and resilience in every area of your life.

Learning to Say No

The ability to say no is essential for establishing healthy boundaries and maintaining balance in life. For Christian businesswomen, this skill often feels challenging, as the desire to help others or seize opportunities can overshadow the need for self-care and alignment with God's purpose. However, saying no is not a rejection of others—it is an act of discernment, enabling women to steward their time, energy, and resources wisely. This practice empowers them to focus on what truly aligns with their God-given calling.

The Spiritual Perspective on Saying No

For Christian businesswomen, saying "no" is not about avoiding responsibility or seeking personal convenience. Instead, it reflects the profound biblical principle of stewardship—wisely managing the resources God has entrusted to us, including time, energy, and talents. Just as a gardener prunes branches to encourage healthier growth and abundant fruit, learning to say no enables us to focus on what truly aligns with God's purpose for our lives.

Saying no is a powerful act of obedience. It ensures that our commitments reflect God's priorities rather than being driven by societal expectations, guilt, or fear of missing out.It allows us to create space for God to work through us, using our time and abilities for endeavors that bear lasting fruit.

Scriptural Anchor:

Matthew 6:33 (NIV):

"But seek first His kingdom and His righteousness, and all these things will be given to you as well."

This verse reminds us to align our actions with God's will above all else. When we prioritize God's kingdom, He faithfully provides for our needs and directs us toward a life that honors Him.

Practical Strategies for Saying No

1. Be Clear and Respectful

Communicating your boundaries effectively requires clarity and kindness. Avoid vague or evasive language that might lead to misunderstandings. Instead, use direct yet respectful words to express your limitations and ensure the other person feels valued.

Example:

"Thank you so much for considering me for this opportunity, but I need to focus on my current priorities and cannot commit at this time. I truly appreciate your understanding."

This approach maintains professionalism and care, preserving relationships while honoring your boundaries and values.

2. Practice in Small Situations

If saying no feels uncomfortable, begin by practicing in less critical scenarios. Declining minor commitments, such as casual social invitations or optional tasks, helps build confidence and assertiveness over time. Each small victory reinforces your ability to set boundaries without guilt.

Example:

A businesswoman declines a non-essential committee role, saying, "I'm honored to be asked, but I need to focus on my current responsibilities right now."

As you grow more comfortable, you'll find it easier to say no in high-stakes situations, preserving energy for what truly matters.

3. Lean on Prayer for Discernment

When making decisions about commitments, Seeking God's guidance is essential. Prayer provides clarity, helping us discern whether an opportunity aligns with God's purpose for our lives.

Reflect on:

Proverbs 3:5-6 (NIV):

"Trust in the Lord with all your heart and lean not on your own understanding; in all your ways submit to Him, and He will make your paths straight."

Before responding to a request, pause to pray for wisdom:

"Lord, guide my thoughts and decisions. Help me to prioritize what aligns with Your will and let go of anything that distracts me from serving You."

This prayerful pause creates space for divine insight, ensuring that your yes is meaningful and your no is intentional.

Examples of Saying No with Grace and Purpose

1. **In Professional Settings:**

   Imagine being asked to take on an additional project when your workload is already overwhelming. Instead of over-

committing, you might say:
"I appreciate your trust in me, but my current workload prevents me from taking this on. I'd be happy to recommend someone else who might be able to help."

2. **In Personal Relationships:**
When asked to attend a social event that conflicts with your rest or family time, consider responding:
"Thank you for inviting me! Unfortunately, I have other commitments during that time, but I hope it goes wonderfully."

The Freedom Found in Saying No

Learning to say no is liberating. It frees Christian businesswomen from the weight of unnecessary obligations and enables them to channel their energy into pursuits that truly align with their values and God's calling. This intentional focus leads to a life of greater fulfillment and impact, allowing women to serve effectively without sacrificing their well-being.

Reflection Verse:

Galatians 5:1 (NIV):

"It is for freedom that Christ has set us free. Stand firm, then, and do not let yourselves be burdened again by a yoke of slavery."

This verse encourages us to embrace the freedom that comes from living in alignment with God's purpose, unhindered by the chains of overcommitment or misplaced priorities.

Conclusion: Saying No to Say Yes to God

Saying no is not about rejecting others but about making room to say yes to God. By practicing discernment and prioritizing what aligns with His will, Christian businesswomen can experience balance, joy, and purpose. Each no becomes a step toward a life that reflects faith, focus, and intentionality, contributing to God's kingdom while maintaining personal peace.

Embrace the courage to say no, knowing that it will lead to a meaningful and God-honoring life. As you lean on Him for guidance, let your decisions reflect the wisdom and grace that come from walking in His purpose.

Prioritizing Self-Care: A Biblical Stewardship

Self-care is a vital practice rooted in the biblical principle of stewardship, emphasizing the importance of nurturing the body, mind, and spirit. As Christian women, understanding that our bodies are temples of the Holy Spirit (1 Corinthians 6:19-20) reframes self-care as an act of worship and preparation for serving God and others. It is not selfish but a necessary foundation for living a life of purpose, faith, and effectiveness.

1. Set Boundaries Around Rest

God Himself modeled the importance of rest when He ceased work on the seventh day of creation. Rest is not only a command but a gift—a sacred opportunity to restore both our physical and spiritual well-being.

Example:

Dedicate one day each week as a Sabbath for worship, reflection, and renewal. Use this time to disconnect from work-related pressures and focus on deepening your relationship with God.

Scriptural Guidance: Exodus 20:8-10 (NIV): *"Remember the Sabbath day by keeping it holy. Six days you shall labor and do all your work, but the seventh day is a Sabbath to the Lord your God."*

Practical Application:

- Turn off work emails and notifications on your Sabbath.
- Spend time in nature, reflecting on God's creation and bless-

ings.

- Create a family tradition of sharing prayers or reflections at the end of the day.

2. Engage in Mindfulness Practices

Mindfulness helps Christian women remain present in God's promises and connect deeply with His presence. Practices such as prayer, meditation, and scripture reflection encourage a mindset grounded in faith, reducing stress and promoting inner peace.

Example:

Start each morning with quiet time, reflecting on a scripture that inspires you. Pair this practice with intentional breathing or journaling to center your thoughts.

Scriptural Guidance: Philippians 4:13 (NIV): *"I can do all this through Him who gives me strength."*

Practical Application:

- Meditate on a verse like Psalm 46:10: "Be still, and know that I am God."

- Practice gratitude by listing three things you are thankful for each day.

- Use prayer pauses throughout your day to recalibrate and reconnect with God.

3. Focus on Physical Health

A healthy body supports a resilient spirit. Prioritizing regular exercise, quality sleep, and balanced nutrition equips Christian women to handle life's demands while honoring the gift of health God has entrusted to them.

Example:

Incorporate physical activity that you enjoy, such as walking, swimming, or yoga. Use this time as an opportunity for prayer or scripture meditation.

Scriptural Guidance: Psalm 23:1-3 (NIV): The *Lord is my shepherd, I lack nothing. He makes me lie down in green pastures, He leads me beside quiet waters, He refreshes my soul."*

Practical Application:

- Take a brisk walk in the morning while meditating on God's faithfulness.
- Plan nutritious meals that fuel your body and uplift your energy.
- Create a bedtime routine that includes reading scripture or reflecting on the day.

4. Nurture Relationships

Meaningful relationships provide emotional and spiritual nourishment. Surrounding yourself with people who encourage, support, and uplift you fosters a sense of belonging and joy.

Example:

Join a Bible study group or prayer circle where you can share experiences, pray together, and build lasting friendships. These connections serve as a source of strength during challenges and a celebration of shared victories.

Scriptural Guidance: Hebrews 10:24-25 (NIV): *"And let us consider how we may spur one another on toward love and good deeds, not giving up meeting together, as some are in the habit of doing, but encouraging one another—and all the more as you see the Day approaching."*

Practical Application:

- Schedule regular coffee dates or walks with trusted friends for connection and encouragement.
- Use social gatherings as opportunities to reflect God's love through kindness and hospitality.
- Pray with family or friends during challenging seasons, leaning on collective faith for strength.

The Impact of Prioritizing Self-Care

When Christian women prioritize self-care, they align themselves with God's design for holistic well-being. This practice enables them to serve their families, communities, and workplaces with renewed energy and purpose. By wisely stewarding their bodies and minds, they honor God and create a ripple effect of positivity and inspiration in their spheres of influence.

Reflection Verse:3 John 1:2 (NIV): *"Dear friend, I pray that you may enjoy good health and that all may go well with you, even as your soul is getting along well."*

Through intentional self-care, Christian women can embody strength and grace from nurturing their mind, body, and spirit, shining as lights in the world.

Prioritizing Self-Care: A Biblical Stewardship

Self-care is a vital practice rooted in the biblical principle of stewardship, emphasizing the importance of nurturing the body, mind, and spirit. As Christian women, understanding that our bodies are temples of the Holy Spirit (1 Corinthians 6:19-20) reframes self-care as an act of worship and preparation for serving God and others. It is not selfish but a necessary foundation for living a life of purpose, faith, and effectiveness.

1. Set Boundaries Around Rest

God Himself modeled the importance of rest when He ceased work on the seventh day of creation. Rest is not only a command but a gift—a sacred opportunity to restore both our physical and spiritual well-being.

Example:

Dedicate one day each week as a Sabbath for worship, reflection, and renewal. Use this time to disconnect from work-related pressures and focus on deepening your relationship with God.

Scriptural Guidance: Exodus 20:8-10 (NIV): *"Remember the Sabbath day by keeping it holy. Six days you shall labor and do all your work, but the seventh day is a Sabbath to the Lord your God."*

Practical Application:

- Turn off work emails and notifications on your Sabbath.
- Spend time in nature, reflecting on God's creation and blessings.
- Create a family tradition of sharing prayers or reflections at the end of the day.

2. Engage in Mindfulness Practices

Mindfulness helps Christian women remain present in God's promises and connect deeply with His presence. Practices such as prayer, meditation, and scripture reflection encourage a mindset grounded in faith, reducing stress and promoting inner peace.

Example:

Start each morning with quiet time, reflecting on a scripture that inspires you. Pair this practice with intentional breathing or journaling to center your thoughts.

Scriptural Guidance: Philippians 4:13 (NIV): *"I can do all this through Him who gives me strength."*

Practical Application:

- Meditate on a verse like Psalm 46:10: "Be still, and know that I am God."
- Practice gratitude by listing three things you are thankful for each day.
- Use prayer pauses throughout your day to recalibrate and reconnect with God.

3. Focus on Physical Health

A healthy body supports a resilient spirit. Prioritizing regular exercise, quality sleep, and balanced nutrition equips Christian women to handle life's demands while honoring the gift of health God has entrusted to them.

Example:

Incorporate physical activity that you enjoy, such as walking, swimming, or yoga. Use this time as an opportunity for prayer or scripture meditation.

Scriptural Guidance: Psalm 23:1-3 (NIV): *"The Lord is my shepherd, I lack nothing. He makes me lie down in green pastures, He leads me beside quiet waters, He refreshes my soul."*

Practical Application:

- Take a brisk walk in the morning while meditating on God's faithfulness.
- Plan nutritious meals that fuel your body and uplift your energy.
- Create a bedtime routine that includes reading scripture or

reflecting on the day.

4. Nurture Relationships

Meaningful relationships provide emotional and spiritual nourishment. Surrounding yourself with people who encourage, support, and uplift you fosters a sense of belonging and joy.

Example:

Join a Bible study group or prayer circle where you can share experiences, pray together, and build lasting friendships. These connections serve as a source of strength during challenges and a celebration of shared victories.

Scriptural Guidance: Hebrews 10:24-25 (NIV): *"And let us consider how we may spur one another on toward love and good deeds, not giving up meeting together, as some are in the habit of doing, but encouraging one another—and all the more as you see the Day approaching."*

Practical Application:

- Schedule regular coffee dates or walks with trusted friends for connection and encouragement.
- Use social gatherings as opportunities to reflect God's love through kindness and hospitality.
- Pray with family or friends during challenging seasons, leaning on collective faith for strength.

The Impact of Prioritizing Self-Care

When Christian women prioritize self-care, they align themselves with God's design for holistic well-being. This practice enables them to serve their families, communities, and workplaces with renewed energy and purpose. By wisely stewarding their bodies and minds, they honor God and spread positivity and inspiration in their spheres of influence.

Reflection Verse:3 John 1:2 (NIV): *"Dear friend, I pray that you may enjoy good health and that all may go well with you, even as your soul is getting along well."*

By practicing intentional self-care, Christian women can embody the strength and grace that stem from a well-nurtured mind, body, and spirit, thereby shining as lights in the world.Setting boundaries offers clarity, enhances well-being, deepens faith, and positively influences others in the journey of Christian businesswomen.

1. **Clarity and Focus:**
   Boundaries help women focus on God's calling and avoid unnecessary distractions.

2. **Improved Well-Being:**
   By reducing stress and preventing burnout, boundaries contribute to better mental, emotional, and physical health.

3. **Strengthened Faith:**
   Prioritizing time with God fosters spiritual growth and alignment with His will.

4. **Positive Impact on Others:**
   Healthy boundaries model self-respect and encourage others to establish their own limits.

Conclusion: Boundaries That Honor God

In conclusion, setting boundaries is essential for Christian businesswomen to prioritize faith, family, health, and purpose. By identifying stress triggers, learning to say no, and prioritizing self-care, women can align their lives with God's design

for balance and peace, fostering spiritual growth and overall well-being.

Setting boundaries is not about building walls; it's about creating a framework that prioritizes what matters most—faith, family, health, and purpose. By identifying stress triggers, learning to say no, and prioritizing self-care, Christian businesswomen can align their lives with God's design for balance and peace.

As Christian businesswomen set boundaries to prioritize their well-being and align with God's purpose, they heed Jesus' call in Matthew 11:28-30 (NIV): "Come to me, all you who are weary and burdened, and I will give you rest. Take my yoke upon you and learn from me, for I am gentle and humble in heart, and you will find rest for your souls. For my yoke is easy and my burden is light."

In embracing boundaries, we honor God's plan for our lives, find strength in His presence, and create space for His blessings to flow abundantly into every area of our journey.

CHAPTER 8

CULTIVATING A MINDFUL WORK ENVIRONMENT

Creating a Calm and Spiritual Workspace: A Guide for Christian Businesswomen

Creating a workspace that exudes calm is essential for productivity, mental well-being, and spiritual growth. For Christian businesswomen, the workspace is more than just a place to complete tasks—it can be a sanctuary for prayer, reflection, and mindful work. A thoughtfully designed space helps reduce stress, improve focus, and foster a deeper connection with God. By intentionally blending functionality with faith, women can create an environment that inspires clarity, creativity, and peace.

The Importance of an Organized Workspace

An impeccably organized workspace is indispensable, not only for visual appeal but as a cornerstone for mental clarity, emotional equilibrium, and heightened productivity. Studies consistently highlight the link between clutter and heightened stress levels. For Christian businesswomen, an organized workspace becomes a tangible representation of biblical values like order, stewardship, and intentional living.

Clutter and Its Impact

Clutter can create a sense of chaos that clouds the mind and hinders productivity. It often leads to unnecessary distractions, making it harder to focus on tasks and increasing feelings of overwhelm. By creating a clean, intentional workspace that is aligned with personal and professional goals, you set the stage for spiritual and practical success.

Scriptural Guidance:

1 Corinthians 14:40 (NIV):

"But everything should be done in a fitting and orderly way."

This verse reminds us that God values order, and by intentionally structuring our workspaces, we embody the principles of harmony and purpose that He values in every aspect of our lives.

Steps to Organize Your Workspace

1. Declutter Regularly:

Regular decluttering removes visual chaos and establishes a fresh environment for productivity. Begin by removing items that no longer serve a purpose or contribute to your work.

- **Action Tip:** Schedule a weekly decluttering session to sort through papers, office supplies, and digital files.

- **Example:** A Christian entrepreneur dedicates Friday afternoons to tidying her desk, ensuring a fresh start for the following week. During this time, she reflects on Psalm 51:10 (NIV):
  "Create in me a pure heart, O God, and renew a steadfast spirit within me."

2. Designate Zones:

Separate areas for specific tasks, such as work, prayer, and reflection, can enhance focus and spiritual balance.

- **Action Tip:** Create a small corner of your desk or workspace as a prayer area, complete with a Bible, a candle, or a cross. This space can remind you to pause and seek God's guidance throughout the day.

- **Example:** A businesswoman sets up her prayer zone with her favorite scripture, Jeremiah 29:11 (NIV):
"For I know the plans I have for you," declares the Lord, "plans to prosper you and not to harm you, plans to give you hope and a future."

3. Incorporate Storage Solutions:

A well-organized system for storing files, office supplies, and personal items reduces stress and saves time. Shelves, bins, and labeled containers can create order and make it easier to maintain a tidy workspace.

- **Action Tip:** Invest in decorative storage options that align with your personal style and inspire joy.

- **Example:** A Christian writer uses labeled bins to organize manuscripts, pairing each with an inspirational quote from Proverbs 16:3 (NIV):
"Commit to the Lord whatever you do, and He will establish your plans."

The Spiritual Impact of an Organized Workspace

An organized workspace does more than just improve efficiency; it creates, improves efficiency, and thrive. For Christian businesswomen, this intentional design reflects stewardship—managing the resources God has provided in a way that honors Him.

Biblical Inspiration:

Luke 16:10 (NIV):

"Whoever can be trusted with very little can also be trusted with much."

By maintaining an organized space, you demonstrate faithfulness in the small tasks, positioning yourself for greater responsibilities and blessings.

Incorporating Faith into Your Workspace

1. Display Scripture Verses:

Frame your favorite Bible verses or write them on sticky notes to keep God's promises front and center.

- **Example:** A financial advisor keeps Philippians 4:13 (NIV)—*"I can do all this through Him who gives me strength"*—on her desk to remind her of God's empowerment during busy days.

2. Create a Prayer Journal Space:

Dedicate an area for writing prayers, gratitude lists, or reflections. This practice integrates mindfulness into your routine and strengthens your connection with God.

- **Example:** Before starting her workday, a marketing executive journals three blessings from the previous day, reflecting on James 1:17 (NIV):
  "Every good and perfect gift is from above."

The Role of Visual Serenity

A workspace without clutter promotes a peaceful visual environment, reducing stress and improving concentration. Personal and faith-inspired touches can make a workspace a haven of calm.

Tips for Creating Visual Serenity:

1. **Incorporate Calming Colors:** Use soothing tones like blues, greens, or neutrals to promote relaxation.

2. **Add Plants or Nature Elements:** Indoor plants not only purify the air but also uplift the spirit.

3. **Limit Visual Noise:** Keep only the essentials on your desk to reduce distractions and maintain focus.

Example: A consultant keeps a single potted peace lily on her desk, meditating on Psalm 23:2 (NIV):

"He makes me lie down in green pastures; He leads me beside quiet waters, He refreshes my soul."

A Daily Practice of Stewardship

Organizing your workspace is not a one-time task; it is an ongoing practice that reflects your commitment to stewardship and intentional living. Each time you tidy, arrange, or curate your environment, you create space for both productivity and spiritual growth.

Reflection Verse:

Colossians 3:23 (NIV):

"Whatever you do, work at it with all your heart, as working for the Lord, not for human masters."

By maintaining an organized workspace, you honor God's presence in your work and create an atmosphere where His peace can flourish.

Final Thought

An organized workspace is more than a practical necessity; it is a sacred space where faith and function meet. By decluttering, designing zones, and incorporating elements of inspiration and serenity, Christian businesswomen can create an environment that supports their professional endeavors and nourishes their spiritual lives.

Lighting: The Impact on Mood and Focus

Lighting plays a pivotal role in shaping our mood, energy levels, and ability to focus. Research confirms that natural light positively affects mental health, enhancing serotonin production, boosting concentration, and reducing feelings of fatigue (Boubekri et al., 2014). For Christian businesswomen, thoughtful lighting can also symbolize God's presence and guidance in daily endeavors, making it a vital aspect of workspace design.

The Benefits of Optimal Lighting

Natural light has profound effects on physical and emotional well-being. Exposure to sunlight regulates circadian rhythms, improving sleep quality and overall mood. In workspaces where natural light is limited, artificial lighting designed to mimic daylight can offer similar benefits. Adjusting the intensity and warmth of your lighting creates a calming and productive environment, essential for navigating the demands of a busy professional life. For instance, softer lighting can promote relaxation during moments of reflection, while brighter lighting is ideal for tasks that require attention to detail.

Biblical Inspiration:

Psalm 119:105 (NIV):

"Your word is a lamp to my feet, a light on my path."

This verse serves as a reminder that just as physical light illuminates our path, God's Word provides spiritual clarity and direction.

Tips for Creating Optimal Lighting

1. Maximize Natural Light

Whenever possible, prioritize natural light in your workspace. Sunlight enhances alertness, elevates mood, and provides a refreshing ambiance.

- **Practical Application:**

  Position your desk near a window to maximize natural light.

Keep curtains or blinds open during the day to let sunlight flood your workspace. If privacy is a concern, consider sheer curtains that diffuse light without blocking it entirely.

- **Example:** A designer sets her desk by a window, using the early morning sunlight as an inspiration for her creative projects. She begins her day by reflecting on Genesis 1:3 (NIV): *"And God said, 'Let there be light,' and there was light."*

2. Use Adjustable Lamps

Adjustable lighting allows you to customize your workspace to suit various tasks and moods. Dim light can be soothing for moments of reflection, while bright light is ideal for detail-oriented work.

- **Practical Application:**
  Choose desk lamps with dimming features or color temperature controls. Warm light creates a cozy atmosphere for evening work, while cooler light can energize you during the day.

- **Example:** A businesswoman working late into the night uses a dimmable lamp to create a gentle, calming glow. During her breaks, she meditates on John 8:12 (NIV):
  "I am the light of the world. Whoever follows me will never walk in darkness, but will have the light of life."

3. Add Accent Lighting

Incorporating decorative lighting enhances the ambiance of your workspace, fostering a sense of peace and comfort. String lights, LED candles, or small accent lamps can add a personal touch while promoting relaxation.

- **Practical Application:**

Place soft accent lighting around your workspace, such as on shelves or a nearby table. These lights can create a warm environment conducive to prayer and reflection.

- **Example:** A Christian entrepreneur decorates her office with string lights and an LED candle on her prayer table. During moments of stress, she pauses to reflect on Matthew 5:16 (NIV):
"Let your light shine before others, that they may see your good deeds and glorify your Father in heaven."

Integrating Faith into Your Lighting Choices

Lighting can be more than a functional element; it can become a visual metaphor for God's guidance and presence in your life. As you design your workspace, let your lighting choices remind you of the spiritual light that illuminates your path.

- **Daily Practice:** Begin your workday by turning on your desk lamp and reciting Psalm 27:1 (NIV):
"The Lord is my light and my salvation—whom shall I fear?"
This simple ritual can set a tone of confidence and trust in God's guidance.

Incorporating intentional lighting can transform your workspace into a sanctuary of focus and tranquility. Whether it's through natural sunlight, adjustable lamps, or accent lights, thoughtful lighting choices promote productivity and spiritual well-being.

Reflection Verse:

2 Corinthians 4:6 (NIV):

"For God, who said, 'Let light shine out of darkness,' made His light shine in our hearts to give us the light of the knowledge of God's glory displayed in the face of Christ."

Surrounding yourself with both physical and spiritual light helps you build a workspace that not only encourages clarity and peace but also fosters a stronger bond with God, creating an environment where spiritual growth and productivity can harmonize.

The Healing Power of Nature

Nature has a deeply calming impact on the mind and body. Incorporating elements of nature into your workspace can reduce stress and foster a sense of well-being. Studies confirm that exposure to plants and natural elements enhances focus, creativity, and emotional health (Bratman et al., 2015). Being surrounded by nature elements can promote mental clarity, inspire creativity, and contribute to emotional well-being, creating a more holistic and uplifting workspace environment.

Ideas for Adding Nature to Your Workspace:

1. **Include Indoor Plants:** Add low-maintenance plants like succulents, ferns, or peace lilies to your desk or shelves.

2. **Use Natural Décor:** incorporate materials like wood, stone, or woven baskets.

3. **Play Nature Sounds:** Use apps or devices to play gentle background sounds, such as ocean waves or bird songs.

Biblical Inspiration: Psalm 19:1 (NIV): *"The heavens declare the glory of God; the skies proclaim the work of His hands."*

Example:

A Christian businesswoman places a small terrarium on her desk and listens to recorded sounds of a flowing river during her morning devotional time. This connection to nature reminds her of God's creation and His presence in every aspect of her work.

Creating a Space for Prayer and Reflection

Incorporating faith into your workspace turns it into a sacred place where spiritual development and work productivity can harmonize. Having a dedicated area for prayer and reflection can provide comfort and direction during challenging moments.

How to Create a Prayer Space:

- **Set Aside a Corner:** Dedicate a small area of your workspace for spiritual practices. Include a devotional, a candle, or a small cross.

- **Use Visual Prompts:** Display a rotating scripture verse or inspirational quotes to meditate on throughout the day.

- **Schedule Prayer Breaks:** Set alarms to remind yourself to pause and seek God's guidance during busy hours.

Biblical Inspiration: Matthew 6:6 (NIV): *"But when you pray, go into your room, close the door and pray to your Father, who is unseen. Then your Father, who sees what is done in secret will reward you."*

Example:

A busy executive begins each workday by lighting a candle in her prayer corner and meditating on Philippians 4:13: *"I can do all this through Him who gives me strength."*

The Role of Boundaries in Workspace Design

Establishing clear boundaries in your workspace is crucial for maintaining balance and reducing stress. These boundaries help differentiate between work and rest, ensuring that neither is compromised.

How to Set Boundaries

1. **Designate Work Hours:** Clearly define when your workday begins and ends, leaving time for rest and family.

2. **Use Physical Cues:** Separate your workspace from relaxation areas with partitions or furniture arrangement.

3. **Incorporate Breaks:** Schedule regular breaks to stretch, breathe, or pray.

Biblical Inspiration: Exodus 20:8-10 (NIV): *"Remember the Sabbath day by keeping it holy."*

Example:

A Christian freelancer sets a strict rule to close her laptop by 6 PM daily, dedicating evenings to family and spiritual renewal.

Encouraging Mindfulness Through Design

Mindfulness in the workspace allows for greater presence, focus, and productivity. By designing a space that encourages mindfulness, women can remain attuned to their tasks while staying grounded in their faith.

Mindfulness Design Tips:

- **Incorporate Aromatherapy:** Use calming scents like lavender or eucalyptus to create a peaceful atmosphere.

- **Add a Visual Focal Point:** Place a piece of artwork or scripture that inspires contemplation.

- **Keep a Gratitude Journal:** Dedicate a notebook for recording daily blessings and answered prayers.

Biblical Inspiration: Colossians 3:23 (NIV): *"Whatever you do, work at it with all your heart, as working for the Lord, not for human masters."*

Example:

During her lunch break, a Christian businesswoman writes three things she is grateful for in her gratitude journal, fostering a mindset of thankfulness that sustains her through the afternoon.

A Sanctuary for Both Work and Faith

Designing a workspace that fosters calm and purpose is more than a practical endeavor—it is an intentional act of merging professional aspirations with spiritual devotion. A thoughtfully curated environment can serve as both a functional area for productivity and a sacred space for communion with God. For Christian businesswomen, this balance provides the clarity and focus needed to navigate their dual responsibilities with grace and intention.

Creating this sanctuary involves mindful choices. Organizing your environment reduces stress and enhances efficiency, while incorporating elements of nature, soft lighting, and personal touches reflects your faith and values. Setting aside a specific area for prayer, scripture meditation, or moments of mindfulness infuses your workday with spiritual nourishment. These practices ground you in God's peace, empowering you to tackle challenges with resilience and confidence.

A Foundation in Scripture

Isaiah 26:3 (NIV) provides a guiding principle for this harmonious workspace:

"You will keep in perfect peace those whose minds are steadfast because they trust in you."

This verse underscores the importance of cultivating an environment that keeps one's mind and heart steadfast in God's presence. By designing a space that prioritizes peace and purpose, one creates a physical and spiritual haven that equips one to face each day's demands with calm assurance.

Practical Applications for Your Sanctuary

1. **Organize with Purpose:**

   Declutter your space regularly, keeping only items that serve your work or inspire you spiritually. Include tools that streamline your workflow and reminders of God's promises, such as framed verses or meaningful symbols.

Example: A businesswoman places a small plaque on her desk engraved with Jeremiah 29:11—*"For I know the plans I have for you," declares the Lord.*

1. **Incorporate Natural Elements:**
   Add plants, flowers, or even a small water feature to your workspace. These elements remind you of God's creation and bring a sense of calm and renewal to your environment.

Example: A single peace lily on a desk can serve as both a natural air purifier and a visual reminder of God's peace.

1. **Set a Spiritual Tone with Lighting:**
   Use warm, soft lighting to create a calming atmosphere. When possible, position your workspace near natural light, allowing sunlight to uplift your mood and help you focus.

Example: Use a lamp with an adjustable dimmer to transition from bright work sessions to a softer ambiance for prayer or reflection.

1. **Establish a Prayer Corner:**
   Dedicate a corner of your workspace to spiritual activities, such as reading scripture, journaling, or praying. To signify this purpose, include items like a Bible, a journal, or a small cross.

Example: Start each morning by journaling a prayer of gratitude in this corner, reflecting on Lamentations 3:22–23—"His *compassions never fail. They are new every morning."*

Final Reflection

Your workspace should mirror your values and priorities by blending productivity with spirituality. When your environment is thoughtfully designed to support both, it becomes more than a place of work—it becomes a sanctuary. This special area enables you to handle your duties with skill, grace, and a strong bond with God.

As you cultivate this sanctuary, let Isaiah 26:3 serve as your anchor:

"You will keep in perfect peace those whose minds are steadfast because they trust in you."

By purposeful design and steadfast faith, you can turn your workspace into a place of peace and meaning, paving the way for achievement, tranquility, and spiritual development.

CHAPTER 9

BUILDING A SUPPORTIVE COMMUNITY

No one is meant to walk the journey of life alone, especially in the demanding and often isolating world of business. For Christian businesswomen, creating a supportive community is more than a beneficial tactic—it reflects God's plan for His people. Scriptural examples, such as the early Christian community in Acts 2:42–47, Paul and Timothy's relationship in 1 Timothy 1:2, and the accountability between James and Peter in Galatians 2:11–14, show how fellowship, accountability, and shared faith strengthen individuals and promote growth. As Proverbs 27:17 (NIV) reminds us, *"As iron sharpens iron, so one person sharpens another."*

This chapter delves into the importance of community in stress management, the strategies for achieving work-life balance, and the significance of spiritual connections in personal and professional growth. Fellowship provides an anchor in times of uncertainty, a source of wisdom when facing challenges, and a space to celebrate victories, big and small. Whether through prayer groups, mentorship relationships, or professional networks, Christian women find in community the encouragement to persevere and the inspiration to thrive.

In the pages ahead, we will uncover practical ways to build a support network, engage with others authentically, and embrace the transformative power of shared experiences. From finding your tribe to sharing your story, this chapter will guide you in creating connections that align with your values and uplift your spirit. Together, we'll see how a community rooted in faith can turn stress into strength and isolation into empowerment.

Let's explore how God uses relationships to shape our paths, sharpen our character, and remind us that we are never alone in our journey.

The Importance of Fellowship in Managing Stress for Christian Businesswomen

For Christian businesswomen balancing work and personal life, fellowship is essential for building resilience. In a world filled with pressures and expectations, a supportive community becomes a sanctuary—a place where burdens are shared, encouragement is given, and faith is strengthened. Research underscores the importance of social support in reducing stress, enhancing mental well-being, and fostering resilience (Cohen & Wills, 1985). For believers, fellowship also becomes a spiritual practice that reinforces God's design for connection and mutual care.

The Bible beautifully highlights the value of community in Ecclesiastes 4:9-10 (NIV):

"Two are better than one, because they have a good return for their labor: If either of them falls down, one can help the other up. But pity anyone who falls and has no one to help them up."

This passage reminds us that life is not meant to be a solitary journey. God created us for connection, and through fellowship, we find the strength to face challenges with grace and perseverance.

The Role of Fellowship in Providing Strength and Peace for Christian Businesswomen

1. Shared Prayer and Spiritual Uplift

A significant aspect of fellowship is the chance to pray collectively. Shared prayer unites hearts in faith, bringing peace and reassurance. When women gather for prayer, they establish a sacred environment where worries are eased and they sense God's presence.

Example: Imagine a small group of businesswomen meeting weekly to pray for each other's professional and personal concerns. As they lift their voices in unison, their collective faith bolsters each individual's strength, reminding them that God is in control.

Scriptural Anchor: Matthew 18:20 (NIV):

"For where two or three gather in my name, there am I with them."

2. Shared Wisdom Through Experiences

Engaging with fellow believers provides an opportunity to learn from one another's experiences. Whether through advice on work-life balance, tips for time management, or insights on spiritual growth, shared wisdom fosters personal and professional development.

For instance, an experienced entrepreneur recounts overcoming challenges with faith and imparts useful tactics to younger group members. Her testimony inspires others to trust God's timing in their own challenges.

Scriptural Anchor: Proverbs 15:22 (NIV):

"Plans fail for lack of counsel, but with many advisers they succeed."

3. Mutual Encouragement and Accountability

Additionally, fellowship encourages accountability, inspiring women to uphold their principles and goals. Through sharing objectives and struggles, participants can support each other in setting boundaries, focusing on self-care, and remaining grounded in their faith.

Example: During a monthly fellowship, one woman admitted to struggling with overcommitting to projects. The group offered support, shared tips on delegation, and committed to holding her accountable for setting realistic boundaries.

Scriptural Anchor: Hebrews 10:24-25 (NIV):

"And let us consider how we may spur one another on toward love and good deeds, not giving up meeting together, as some are in the habit of doing, but encouraging one another—and all the more as you see the Day approaching."

Fellowship in Action: Practical Steps for Christian Businesswomen

1. **Join a Faith-Based Group:** Seek out organizations like Christian Women in Business, Women of Faith in Leadership, or local church groups designed for Christian women in leadership.

2. **Create Space for Connection:** Host or attend small group meetings to discuss faith, work, and life challenges.

3. **Incorporate Prayer:** Make prayer a central part of your fellowship gatherings, lifting up collective and individual concerns to God.

4. **Celebrate Successes Together:** Use fellowship as an opportunity to recognize and celebrate milestones, fostering joy and gratitude.

Conclusion: Strength Through Community

Fellowship is more than a strategy for managing stress—it is a gift from God that strengthens our faith and deepens our resilience. Engaging with others in authentic, faith-centered relationships provides a lifeline during difficult seasons and a source of joy during celebrations.

As Ecclesiastes 4:12 (NIV) reminds us:

"Though one may be overpowered, two can defend themselves. A cord of three strands is not quickly broken."

Through fellowship, we weave our lives together, forming a strong and unbreakable bond that reflects God's love and purpose. When Christian businesswomen embrace the power of community, they find not only support but also the courage to face challenges with grace and faith.

Benefits of Fellowship for Christian Businesswomen

1. Shared Prayer and Spiritual Support

Shared prayer fosters a sense of unity and provides emotional relief. Research conducted by Krause and Hayward in 2013 showed that group prayer enhances spiritual well-being and reduces anxiety.

Example:

Imagine a group of businesswomen meeting weekly for prayer and reflection. As they lift each other's concerns to God, they experience peace and strength through their collective faith.

Scriptural Anchor: Matthew 18:20 (NIV):

"For where two or three gather in my name, there am I with them."

2. Accountability for Balance and Growth

Accountability within a community encourages personal and professional growth. Sharing challenges and successes helps women stay committed to their goals and fosters healthy work-life balance.

Example:

During a monthly meeting, a member shares her struggle with time management. Fellow group members offer practical advice and hold her accountable for implementing changes.

Scriptural Anchor: Proverbs 27:17 (NIV):

"As iron sharpens iron, so one person sharpens another."

Research Support:

Studies show that accountability in groups improves goal adherence and personal development (Zimmerman & Schunk, 2011).

3. Mentorship and Guidance

The community offers opportunities for mentorship, with seasoned businesswomen mentoring others. This environment fosters development, combats isolation, and encourages education.

Example:

A senior entrepreneur mentors a young professional, sharing insights about maintaining faith while growing a business.

Scriptural Anchor: Titus 2:3-4 (NIV):

"Teach the older women to be reverent in the way they live... Then they can urge the younger women to love their husbands and children."

4. Joy and Gratitude

Fellowship encourages celebration and gratitude, which shift focus from stress to appreciation. Gratitude is associated with improved mental health and reduced stress (Emmons & McCullough, 2003).

Example:

A networking group hosts a monthly gratitude session to celebrate achievements and express thankfulness for God's blessings.

Scriptural Anchor: 1 Thessalonians 5:11 (NIV):

"Therefore encourage one another and build each other up, just as in fact you are doing."

Building Meaningful Connections: Navigating Networking with Purpose

Building a network of like-minded individuals is essential for Christian businesswomen seeking to align their professional aspirations with their faith. A strong, faith-centered community not only provides encouragement and support but also nurtures spiritual and personal growth. This intentional networking goes beyond surface-level connections, creating relationships rooted in shared values, mutual respect, and a commitment to uplifting one another.

Proverbs 18:24 (NIV) beautifully underscores the value of meaningful connections:
"Having unreliable friends soon leads to ruin, but there is a friend who sticks closer than a brother."

A carefully cultivated network offers strength, accountability, and wisdom, ensuring that you're surrounded by individuals who inspire, challenge, and empower you to thrive.

Steps to Finding Your Tribe.

1. Define Your Goals

Before seeking out your tribe, clarify what you're looking for in a community. Reflect on qualities such as shared faith, professional alignment, and mutual encouragement. Are you seeking prayer partners, professional mentors, or peers to share your journey? Defining these goals helps you focus on building connections that truly resonate with your values and needs.

Reflection Example:
A businesswoman striving for work-life balance might prioritize finding a group of women who can share faith-based insights on managing responsibilities while staying aligned with God's purpose.

Scriptural Anchor: Amos 3:3 (NIV):

"Do two walk together unless they have agreed to do so?"

2. Engage Locally and Online

Expand your reach by exploring both local and virtual opportunities to connect with like-minded individuals.

- **Locally:** Attend church events, women's ministry meetings, and professional workshops in your area. These gatherings often provide a welcoming environment to meet others who share your faith and goals.

- **Online:** Join social media groups, professional forums, or Christian business networks designed to connect women in leadership. Platforms like LinkedIn, Facebook, and specialized Christian networking sites can be valuable resources.

Example:

A woman seeking mentorship might attend a Christian leadership conference or join an online group for female entrepreneurs. By engaging in discussions and offering insights, she builds relationships with others on similar journeys.

Scriptural Anchor: Hebrews 10:25 (NIV):

"Let us not give up meeting together, as some are in the habit of doing, but encouraging one another—and all the more as you see the Day approaching."

3. Prioritize Reciprocity

Strong relationships are built on mutual support and encouragement. As you engage with others, prioritize helping them while also being willing to accept their support. Networking with a selfless and caring approach builds trust and strengthens relationships.

Practical Tips:

- Offer your skills or resources to support a fellow businesswoman's goals.

- Celebrate others' successes and provide encouragement during challenges.

- Be intentional about following up after initial connections to deepen relationships.

Example:

A graphic designer might offer to help a fellow businesswoman create marketing materials in exchange for advice on time management. This exchange builds trust and sets the foundation for a meaningful partnership.

Scriptural Anchor: Galatians 6:2 (NIV):

"Carry each other's burdens, and in this way, you will fulfill the law of Christ."

Integrating Faith into Networking Practices

Networking with purpose is not just about expanding professional opportunities; it's about aligning your relationships with God's will. Prayer plays a vital role in this process, guiding your decisions and deepening your connections.

Incorporating Prayer into Networking:

- **Pray for Discernment:** Ask God to lead you to individuals who align with His purpose for your life.

- **Pray for the Connection:** Before attending events or engaging online, invite God to bless your interactions.

- **Pray for Your Tribe:** Regularly pray for your network, asking for their growth, success, and spiritual well-being.

Scriptural Anchor: Proverbs 3:5-6 (NIV):

"Trust in the Lord with all your heart and lean not on your own understanding; in all your ways submit to Him, and He will make your paths straight."

Conclusion: The Power of an Aligned Network

Finding your tribe is a journey of intentionality and faith. By defining your goals, engaging purposefully, and prioritizing reciprocity, you can cultivate a community that supports and uplifts you. More than just professional allies, your tribe becomes a source of spiritual encouragement and a reflection of God's design for connection.

As Proverbs 27:17 (NIV) reminds us:

"As iron sharpens iron, so one person sharpens another."

Christian businesswomen can navigate difficulties with assurance, rejoice in victories with delight, and walk their journeys with unwavering faith because they have a tribe that supports them and exemplifies God's love and purpose for their lives.

Sharing Your Journey

Sharing your experiences is a meaningful way to show vulnerability and faith, strengthen bonds within the community, and inspire others. For Christian businesswomen, it serves as a testament to God's faithfulness and a source of encouragement for others navigating similar challenges. Authentic storytelling fosters deeper connections, reinforces trust, and reminds us that we are never alone in our struggles or triumphs.

Psalm 107:2 (NIV) captures the importance of sharing our stories:

"Let the redeemed of the Lord tell their story—those He redeemed from the hand of the foe."

By sharing how God has influenced your life, you not only honor Him but also offer hope and encouragement to others on their paths.

How to Share Your Journey

1. **Be Transparent:** Authenticity is the cornerstone of meaningful connections. When you share your struggles alongside your victories, you build trust and demonstrate the trans-

formative power of faith. Transparency invites others to see God's work in your life, even during the most challenging seasons.

Example:

A woman recounts her experience of starting a business while managing personal hardships. By sharing how prayer and perseverance guided her, she inspires others to lean on their faith during trials.

Scriptural Anchor: 2 Corinthians 12:9 (NIV):

"But he said to me, 'My grace is sufficient for you, for my power is made perfect in weakness.' Therefore I will boast all the more gladly about my weaknesses, so that Christ's power may rest on me."

1. **Highlight Faith:** Your journey is a testimony of God's faithfulness. Sharing how He has guided you through challenges and blessed you in unexpected ways demonstrates His sovereignty and love. This focus on faith encourages others to trust God in their own journeys.

Example:

A businesswoman shares how she relied on Philippians 4:13 (NIV)—*"I can do all this through Him who gives me strength"*—to overcome self-doubt and confidently lead her team. Her testimony encourages others to draw strength from Scripture.

1. **Provide Practical Advice:** Sharing actionable strategies and practices that have helped you in your journey empowers others to overcome similar challenges. By offering practical insights, you create a roadmap for others to follow, blending faith with tangible solutions.

Example:

A woman writes a blog post about overcoming burnout through

prayer, gratitude, and intentional time management. She outlines steps like setting aside morning prayer time, practicing gratitude journaling, and meditating on verses such as Matthew 11:28 (NIV):

"Come to me, all you who are weary and burdened, and I will give you rest."

Her advice equips readers with tools to navigate their own struggles with grace and resilience.

The Impact of Sharing Your Story

1. Inspiring Hope

Your testimony reminds others that God is active and present in every season of life. Whether it's a story of overcoming obstacles or achieving a long-held goal, your journey serves as a beacon of hope.

Scriptural Anchor: Romans 8:28 (NIV):

"And we know that in all things God works for the good of those who love Him, who have been called according to His purpose."

2. Fostering Community

When you share your journey, you create a space where others feel safe to share theirs. This mutual exchange fosters empathy, understanding, and a sense of belonging, strengthening the bonds within your community.

Example:

A group of Christian entrepreneurs hosts a storytelling evening where each person shares a key moment in their faith journey. The event builds trust and inspires collaboration within the group.

3. Glorifying God

Every story of transformation and perseverance ultimately points back to God's goodness. Sharing your journey is an act of worship, reflecting His grace and power to others.

Scriptural Anchor: 1 Peter 2:9 (NIV):

"But you are a chosen people, a royal priesthood, a holy nation, God's

special possession, that you may declare the praises of Him who called you out of darkness into His wonderful light."

Practical Ways to Share Your Journey

- **Social Media:** Share short reflections or testimonies on platforms like LinkedIn or Instagram, incorporating scripture and practical advice.

- **Blogging or Writing:** Create a blog or contribute to publications that align with your faith and professional focus.

- **Speaking Engagements:** Share your story at church events, conferences, or professional workshops.

- **Small Group Discussions:** Open up about your experiences during fellowship meetings to encourage deeper conversations.

Conclusion: Inspiring Through Authentic Storytelling

Sharing your journey is a gift—not just for those who hear it but for yourself as well. It reinforces your faith, builds connections, and brings glory to God. Whether you're sharing a small success or a significant change, your story can uplift and motivate others.

As Psalm 96:3 (NIV) reminds us:

"Declare His glory among the nations, His marvelous deeds among all peoples."

By openly sharing your experiences, you become a channel for God's love, inspiring others to rely on Him in their own lives and creating a supportive community based on faith and mutual support. By boldly sharing your experiences, you become a vessel for God's light, encouraging others to trust Him in their own lives and building a supportive community grounded in faith and mutual encouragement.

The Power of Community in Stress Management

Juggling work duties and personal obligations can be daunting for Christian businesswomen. In these moments, the power of community becomes a vital source of strength and renewal. Fellowship with like-minded believers offers a safe haven where burdens are shared, faith is reinforced, and resilience is cultivated.

The Bible highlights the transformative role of community in Hebrews 10:24-25 (NIV):

"And let us consider how we may spur one another on toward love and good deeds, not giving up meeting together, as some are in the habit of doing, but encouraging one another—and all the more as you see the Day approaching."

This passage emphasizes that community is more than just connection—it involves actively supporting each other to strengthen faith and love, even during life's challenges.

How Community Reduces Stress

1. A Safe Space to Share

Fellowship creates a supportive environment where women can openly discuss their challenges, fears, and victories. This act of sharing not only lightens emotional burdens but also fosters a sense of belonging, reminding women that they are not alone in their struggles.

Example:

During a women's fellowship meeting, a businesswoman shares her challenges in maintaining work-life balance. Others offer empathy, advice, and prayer, creating a sense of solidarity that eases her stress.

Scriptural Anchor: Galatians 6:2 (NIV):

"Carry each other's burdens, and in this way, you will fulfill the law of Christ."

2. Encouragement Through Prayer and Accountability

Community provides a network of prayer warriors who lift each other up during difficult times. Regular gatherings encourage accountability, helping women stay aligned with their spiritual and professional goals.

Example:

A group of entrepreneurs commits to praying for each other's business challenges. One member shares her struggles with self-doubt, and the group prays over her, reminding her of God's promises.

Scriptural Anchor: James 5:16 (NIV):

"Therefore confess your sins to each other and pray for each other so that you may be healed. The prayer of a righteous person is powerful and effective."

3. Building Resilience Through Shared Wisdom

Engaging with a community of believers allows women to draw from one another's experiences and insights. Whether it's advice on managing stress or navigating workplace dynamics, shared wisdom strengthens resilience and fosters growth.

Example:

A seasoned business leader shares her strategy for handling stressful deadlines by setting aside dedicated prayer time. Her testimony inspires others to adopt similar practices.

Scriptural Anchor: Proverbs 11:14 (NIV):

"For lack of guidance a nation falls, but victory is won through many advisers."

The Joy of Fellowship

Fellowship doesn't just alleviate stress; it cultivates joy and gratitude by focusing on God's faithfulness and celebrating His blessings. Gathering with others to worship, share testimonies, or celebrate milestones shifts the focus from challenges to appreciation.

Example:

A small group organizes a gratitude dinner, during which each member shares one way God has blessed them in the past month. This practice strengthens their faith and creates a positive, uplifting atmosphere.

Scriptural Anchor: 1 Thessalonians 5:16-18 (NIV):

"Rejoice always, pray continually, give thanks in all circumstances; for this is God's will for you in Christ Jesus."

Key Strategies for Building Community to Manage Stress include fostering a culture of gratitude and encouragement.

1. **Participate in Prayer Circles:** Regularly join or create prayer circles focused on supporting each other's needs.

2. **Host Fellowship Events:** Organize gatherings that foster meaningful conversations, shared worship, and mutual encouragement.

3. **Engage in Service Together:** Collaborate on community service projects, which not only alleviate stress but also strengthen bonds and reflect God's love.

Conclusion: The Transformative Power of Fellowship for Christian Businesswomen

Community is God's gift to His people, offering strength, encouragement, and joy in every season of life. For Christian businesswomen, fellowship is more than a support system—it is a source of spiritual renewal and a reminder of God's unchanging faithfulness.

As Proverbs 27:17 (NIV) reminds us:

"As iron sharpens iron, so one person sharpens another."

By investing in relationships that align with their faith, women can manage stress with grace, celebrate life's blessings with gratitude, and inspire one another to pursue love and good deeds. In doing so, they create a ripple effect of encouragement, transforming not only their lives but also the lives of those they touch.

CHAPTER 10

SUSTAINING MINDFULNESS IN EVERYDAY LIFE

Chapter 9: Sustaining Mindfulness in Everyday Life

Mindfulness, which involves being fully focused and attentive, is a powerful tool that helps Christian businesswomen navigate life's challenges with clarity, balance, and grace. Incorporating mindfulness into everyday routines helps women strengthen their bond with God, build emotional strength, and improve their leadership and service skills. This chapter explores how to sustain mindfulness through practical strategies, biblical insights, and inspirational examples.

Creating a Mindfulness Routine

It fosters mental clarity, alleviates stress, and aligns daily actions with God's will. For Christian businesswomen, this routine becomes a sacred space to reconnect with God and navigate challenges with grace.

Step 1: Set Intentional Times for Mindfulness

Mindfulness thrives in intentionality. Identify key moments in your day—morning, midday, or evening—to practice stillness, prayer, and reflection. Consistency in these times helps nurture a rhythm of mindfulness amidst life's demands.

Example: Prior to finalizing a significant contract or undertaking a new project, take a moment to seek God's guidance through prayer, aligning your decisions with His will. Reflect on the wisdom of scripture:

Proverbs 16:3 (NIV):

"Commit to the Lord whatever you do, and he will establish your plans."

By surrendering your plans to God in prayer, you invite His wisdom and peace to shape your decisions and ensure they align with His purpose for your life.

Active Listening: Building Stronger Connections

Mindfulness in decision-making includes the practice of active listening. By being fully present in conversations, you demonstrate respect, empathy, and a Christ-like love for others.

Example:

During a meeting or negotiation, focus entirely on the speaker's words rather than planning your response prematurely. Take a moment to mentally summarize their key points to ensure understanding. Reflect on:

James 1:19 (NIV):

"Everyone should be quick to listen, slow to speak, and slow to become angry."

This mindful approach promotes trust, collaboration, and mutual understanding, setting a foundation for meaningful and effective communication.

Managing Stress in High-Stakes Decisions

Stress is inevitable when making important decisions. Mindfulness techniques, such as deep breathing and grounding exercises, can help you remain calm, focused, and spiritually centered, allowing you to make clear and thoughtful choices.

Example:

Before delivering a crucial presentation or signing an important deal, take five deep breaths to center yourself. As you exhale, meditate on:

Philippians 4:6-7 (NIV):

"Do not be anxious about anything, but in every situation, by prayer and petition, with thanksgiving, present your requests to God. And the peace of God, which transcends all understanding, will guard your hearts and your minds in Christ Jesus."

This practice not only alleviates anxiety but also strengthens your reliance on God's peace, enabling you to approach challenges with confidence and grace.

Integrating Mindfulness into Daily Decisions

Mindfulness becomes most impactful when it is woven into everyday decision-making processes. Practical ways to achieve this include:

- **Starting Meetings with Prayer or Silence:** Dedicate a moment to seek God's guidance and set a positive tone for discussions.

- **Using Scriptural Anchors for Guidance:** Turn to verses like **Proverbs 3:5-6 (NIV):**
  "Trust in the Lord with all your heart and lean not on your own understanding; in all your ways submit to Him, and He will make your paths straight."

- **Taking Mindful Breaks:** Pause periodically throughout the day to reflect, breathe, and reset, ensuring you stay aligned with your goals and faith.

The Long-Term Impact of Mindful Decision-Making

Incorporating mindfulness into your decisions yields profound benefits, both personally and professionally:

1. **Enhanced Clarity:** Mindfulness fosters a calm, focused mindset that enables thoughtful and intentional decisions.

2. **Stronger Relationships:** Active listening and empathy build trust and collaboration in both work and personal spheres.

3. **Resilience and Peace:** By anchoring decisions in prayer and mindfulness, you will develop the strength to navigate challenges confidently.

4. **Faith-Centered Leadership:** Mindful decision-making reflects God's wisdom and grace, inspiring others and glorifying Him in your work.

A Faith-Filled Journey

As Christian businesswomen, embracing mindfulness in your decision-making reflects your trust in God's guidance and your commitment to lead with purpose and integrity. By pausing to pray, listening with intention, and managing stress mindfully, you create a life and career that honor God's will.

Final Reflection:Colossians 3:17 (NIV):

"And whatever you do, whether in word or deed, do it all in the name of the Lord Jesus, giving thanks to God the Father through him."

Let mindfulness serve as a bridge between your faith and your professional endeavors. It will empower you to make decisions with clarity, compassion, and a steadfast trust in God's sovereignty. Through this practice, you will not only navigate your journey with grace but also inspire others to walk in faith and mindfulness.

The Long-Term Benefits of Mindfulness

Sustained mindfulness offers transformative benefits that extend beyond stress reduction, enhancing every aspect of life for Christian businesswomen.

Reduced Anxiety and Enhanced Resilience

Mindfulness helps regulate emotions, reducing anxiety and increasing the ability to adapt to challenges.

Example:

A woman navigating a career setback uses mindfulness to focus on opportunities rather than obstacles. She meditates on **Romans 8:28 (NIV)**:

"And we know that in all things God works for the good of those who love him, who have been called according to his purpose."

Improved Relationships

Mindfulness fosters empathy and compassion, strengthening personal and professional connections.

Example:

Reflect on **Ephesians 4:32 (NIV)**:

"Be kind and compassionate to one another, forgiving each other, just as in Christ God forgave you."

Greater Creativity and Focus

Regular mindfulness practice enhances focus and encourages innovative thinking.

Example:

A creative professional facing a block takes a mindfulness break, meditating on **Ecclesiastes 3:1 (NIV)**:

"There is a time for everything, and a season for every activity under the heavens."

Deepened Faith and Spiritual Growth

Mindfulness reinforces a reliance on God, fostering spiritual maturity.

Example:

Through daily mindfulness routines, a woman strengthens her faith, meditating on **Matthew 11:28-30 (NIV)**:

"Come to me, all you who are weary and burdened, and I will give you rest."

Living a Mindful Life in Christ

Living mindfully as a Christian businesswoman means aligning your actions, thoughts, and decisions with God's purpose, beyond simply handling daily challenges. It involves cultivating an awareness of His presence in every moment, allowing that awareness to shape how you respond to challenges, interact with others, and carry out your work. When mindfulness is deeply rooted in faith, it becomes a powerful tool to honor God, nurture personal growth, and cultivate resilience.

The Foundation of a Christ-Centered Mindful Life

Mindfulness in Christ begins with understanding that our lives are not separate from our spiritual walk. Every task, decision, and interaction is an opportunity to reflect God's love and purpose. Recognizing this turns everyday actions into meaningful acts of worship, making mindfulness a spiritual endeavor.

Scriptural Anchor:

Colossians 3:17 (NIV):

"And whatever you do, whether in word or deed, do it all in the name of the Lord Jesus, giving thanks to God the Father through him."

This verse underscores the essence of living a mindful life in Christ. Whether responding to emails, leading a meeting, or managing personal responsibilities, every action can be a reflection of faith when done with intentionality and gratitude.

Practical Steps for Mindful Living in Christ

1. Begin Your Day with God

Starting the day in communion with God sets the tone for mindful living. Dedicate the first moments of your morning to prayer, reflection, and scripture meditation. This practice centers your mind on His promises and invites His presence into your day.

Example:

Before reaching for your phone, spend five minutes in quiet prayer. Meditate on **Psalm 118:24 (NIV):**

"This is the day the Lord has made; let us rejoice and be glad in it."

As you breathe deeply, thank God for the day ahead and ask for His guidance and peace.

2. Practice Gratitude Throughout the Day

Gratitude shifts your focus from what is lacking to what is abundant, fostering a mindset of contentment and trust in God's provision. Make it a habit to pause and acknowledge His blessings, even in challenging moments.

Example:

During a busy workday, take a moment to jot down three things you're grateful for. Reflect on **1 Thessalonians 5:16-18 (NIV):**

"Rejoice always, pray continually, and give thanks in all circumstances; for this is God's will for you in Christ Jesus."

3. Embrace Mindful Decision-Making

Before making decisions, pause to seek God's guidance. Reflect on your personal values and how each decision aligns with God's specific purpose for your life.

Example:

When faced with a challenging business decision, take a moment to pray for wisdom. Meditate on **Proverbs 3:5-6 (NIV):**

"Trust in the Lord with all your heart and lean not on your own understanding; in all your ways submit to Him, and He will make your paths straight."

This practice reduces impulsivity and ensures that one's actions align with one's faith, leading to decisions that reflect one's values and beliefs.

4. Incorporate Moments of Stillness

In a world that demands constant productivity, intentionally pausing to reconnect with God can be transformative. These moments of stillness allow you to recalibrate your mind and spirit, reducing stress and enhancing focus.

Example:

Set a timer to pause for five minutes of quiet reflection during your day. Close your eyes, take deep breaths, and reflect on **Psalm 46:10 (NIV):**

"Be still, and know that I am God."

5. Infuse Faith into Your Work

Commit every task to God to transform your work into an act of worship. When approached with faith and purpose, even routine tasks can glorify Him.

Example:

Before starting your workday, pray over your to-do list, asking for clarity and efficiency. Reflect on **Ecclesiastes 9:10 (NIV):**

"Whatever your hand finds to do, do it with all your might."

The Transformative Impact of Mindfulness in Christ

1. Resilience in Challenges

Mindfulness grounded in faith enables you to gracefully navigate challenges and obstacles. By focusing on God's sovereignty, you can transform obstacles into opportunities for growth and reliance on His strength.

Example:

During a difficult project, remind yourself of **Romans 8:28 (NIV):** "And we know that in all things God works for the good of those who love Him, who have been called according to His purpose."

This perspective fosters hope and perseverance.

2. Deeper Relationships

Mindfulness enhances one's ability to listen and engage with others, fostering meaningful connections. Being fully engaged in conversations allows you to reflect Christ's love and care.

Example:

When a colleague shares their struggles, give them your undivided attention. Reflect on **Ephesians 4:32 (NIV):**

"Be kind and compassionate to one another, forgiving each other, just as in Christ God forgave you."

3. Clarity and Focus

Practicing mindfulness helps you gain mental clarity, prioritize effectively, and align your efforts with God's calling.

Example:

Use a mindfulness practice, such as journaling or deep breathing, before starting a new project. Focus on **Philippians 4:13 (NIV):**

"I can do all this through Him who gives me strength."

Final Reflection on Living Mindfully in Christ

Mindfulness in Christ is a journey of constant growth and renewal. It is an invitation to live fully in the present while keeping your heart aligned with God's eternal purpose. Incorporating mindfulness into your daily life cultivates peace, purpose, and joy, shining as a source of inspiration to others.

Closing Scripture:

Isaiah 26:3 (NIV):

"You will keep in perfect peace those whose minds are steadfast, because they trust in you."

Let mindfulness guide you closer to God, allowing His presence to shape your thoughts, actions, and aspirations. As you embrace this practice, you not only enrich your own life but also glorify Him in all you do, inspiring others to pursue a life of intentionality and faith.

CHAPTER 11

PRAYER AS A MINDFULNESS PRACTICE

Prayer is not just a spiritual obligation; it is a transformative act that connects the soul with God's presence. For Christian businesswomen who balance demanding careers and personal responsibilities, prayer serves as a sanctuary of mindfulness, offering peace, clarity, and strength. Incorporating prayer into daily routines can help women find stability in chaotic times and cultivate a faith-centered approach to life and work.

This chapter examines prayer as a mindfulness practice. It explores its various forms, the process of developing a prayer habit, and the significant impact of listening to God during moments of stillness.

Prayer as Mindfulness: A Biblical Foundation

Prayer naturally connects with mindfulness by promoting focus on the present moment and intentionality. It is an opportunity to pause, reflect, and acknowledge God's sovereignty, even in the busiest seasons of life. The Bible emphasizes this stillness and intentional connection:

Psalm 46:10 (NIV):

"Be still, and know that I am God."

This verse reminds believers of the power of quiet communion with God, encouraging them to find strength and clarity in His presence.

Prayer as mindfulness encourages Christian businesswomen to shift their focus from the overwhelming demands of the future or the regrets of the past to the blessings and opportunities of the present.

Different Forms of Prayer

Prayer is a sacred dialogue that opens the heart to God's presence, fostering spiritual growth, emotional healing, and a deeper sense of peace. For Christian businesswomen, prayer serves as both a refuge and a source of strength, enabling them to navigate the complexities of their professional and personal lives with clarity and grace. Each form of prayer offers unique opportunities for mindfulness and connection, allowing believers to draw closer to God in every circumstance.

1. Conversational Prayer: A Personal Dialogue with God

Conversational prayer is a personal and informal way to communicate with God. It transforms routine moments into opportunities for meaningful engagement, making God a part of every aspect of life.

Example:

Before a high-stakes presentation, a businesswoman might pray:

"Lord, I need Your wisdom and calmness. Guide my words and let my actions reflect Your love and grace."

Scriptural Anchor:

Philippians 4:6-7 (NIV):

"Do not be anxious about anything, but in every situation, by prayer and petition, with thanksgiving, present your requests to God. And the peace of God, which transcends all understanding, will guard your hearts and your minds in Christ Jesus."

Conversational prayer encourages believers to approach God with openness and honesty, turning everyday challenges into sacred moments of trust and reliance.

2. Gratitude Prayer: Cultivating a Heart of Thankfulness

Gratitude prayer helps shift the focus from challenges to blessings, nurturing a mindset of joy and abundance. It aligns the heart with God's goodness and reinforces His faithfulness.

Example:

At the end of the day, reflect on three blessings:

- A colleague's encouraging words.
- Completing a challenging task.
- The beauty of nature during your commute.

Scriptural Anchor:

1 Thessalonians 5:16-18 (NIV):

"Rejoice always, pray continually, give thanks in all circumstances; for this is God's will for you in Christ Jesus."

Gratitude prayer transforms even the smallest joys into reminders of God's provision, building emotional resilience and fostering contentment.

Pro Tip: Keep a gratitude journal to record daily blessings, creating a tangible reminder of God's faithfulness. Reflecting on these blessings can uplift your spirit, increase your awareness of God's provision, and foster a heart of gratitude in all circumstances.

3. Intercessory Prayer: Uplifting Others

Intercessory prayer emphasizes selflessness, inviting believers to bring the needs of others before God. It fosters empathy and strengthens the bonds of community, reminding us of our interconnectedness in Christ.

Example:

Pray for a colleague struggling with a personal loss:
"Lord, comfort [Name] during this difficult time. Grant them peace, strength, and the assurance of Your love."

Scriptural Anchor:

James 5:16 (NIV):

"Therefore confess your sins to each other and pray for each other so that you may be healed. The prayer of a righteous person is powerful and effective."

Interceding for others not only impacts their lives but also draws us closer to God, aligning our hearts with His compassion and mercy.

4. Contemplative Prayer: Embracing Stillness

Contemplative prayer invites believers to enter into silence and stillness, creating space to listen for God's voice. It aligns with mindfulness by encouraging intentional presence and surrender.

Example:

Practice a simple breath prayer during a moment of stress:

- **Inhale:** "Be still,"

- **Exhale:** "And know that I am God."

Scriptural Anchor:

Psalm 46:10 (NIV):

"Be still, and know that I am God."

Contemplative prayer fosters inner peace and spiritual clarity, enabling believers to find strength and focus in the busyness of life. It reminds us that God's presence transcends the noise of the world, offering a quiet refuge for the soul.

Incorporating Prayer into Daily Life

Prayer is not confined to specific times or locations; it can be a consistent thread woven throughout daily life. Here's how Christian businesswomen can integrate prayer into their routines:

- **Morning Devotion:** Begin the day with a prayer of gratitude and guidance, reflecting on **Psalm 143:8 (NIV):**
  "Let the morning bring me word of your unfailing love, for I have put my trust in you."

- **Midday Pause:** Take a short break to pray for wisdom and strength, meditating on **Isaiah 40:31 (NIV):**
  "But those who hope in the Lord will renew their strength. They will soar on wings like eagles; they will run and not grow weary, they will walk and not be faint."

- **Evening Reflection:** End the day with a prayer of thanksgiving and surrender, echoing **Matthew 11:28 (NIV):**
  "Come to me, all you who are weary and burdened, and I will

give you rest."

Conclusion: The Transformative Power of Prayer

Each form of prayer offers a unique pathway to mindfulness, providing Christian businesswomen with tools to navigate life's challenges while staying deeply connected to God. Whether through open dialogue, gratitude, intercession, or stillness, prayer enriches the spirit and aligns the heart with God's purpose.

Final Reflection:

Colossians 4:2 (NIV):

"Devote yourselves to prayer, being watchful and thankful."

By embracing the multifaceted practice of prayer, you create a life rooted in faith, resilience, and gratitude. Let prayer be your constant companion, guiding you toward peace, purpose, and a deeper connection with the One who sustains you.

Developing a Prayer Habit: Strengthening Your Connection with God

Developing a regular prayer routine is impactful for Christian businesswomen who manage the challenges of life and work. Prayer creates a foundation for mindfulness, fosters inner peace, and deepens one's relationship with God. Through prayer, one can approach each day with purpose, resilience, and faith.

1. Identify Specific Prayer Times

Consistency is key to building a sustainable prayer habit. Choose intentional times during the day that align with your schedule and energy levels. Morning prayers set the tone for the day, midday prayers provide a reset, and evening prayers offer time for reflection and gratitude.

Example:

Start your day with a prayer that dedicates your work and efforts to God.

Scriptural Anchor:

Psalm 5:3 (NIV):

"In the morning, Lord, you hear my voice; in the morning I lay my requests before you and wait expectantly."

- **Morning:** Ask God for guidance and strength for the tasks ahead.
- **Midday:** Pause for a moment of gratitude and reflection.
- **Evening:** Thank God for His provision and surrender the day's challenges to Him.

Tip: Use alarms or reminders to establish a consistent rhythm of prayer throughout the day. Setting reminders can help you stay focused, maintain a prayerful mindset despite busyness, and prioritize moments of connection with God.

2. Create a Sacred Space

Designating a physical space for prayer can enhance focus and reverence. This space should be free from distractions and tailored to inspire peace and connection with God.

Example:

Set up a prayer corner in your office or home. Include a Bible, a journal, and decor like candles or framed scripture.

Scriptural Inspiration:

Jeremiah 29:11 (NIV):

"For I know the plans I have for you," declares the Lord, "plans to prosper you and not to harm you, plans to give you hope and a future."

- Add personal touches like a photo of loved ones or an item that reminds you of God's blessings.
- Keep this space tidy and inviting, so it feels like a sanctuary where you can commune with God.

3. Use Prayer Prompts

Prayer prompts guide your thoughts and deepen your focus, especially on busy or overwhelming days. Scripture, written prayers, or gratitude lists can serve as starting points for meaningful dialogue with God.

Example:

Reflect on this verse during stressful moments:

Matthew 11:28 (NIV):

"Come to me, all you who are weary and burdened, and I will give you rest."

- **Gratitude Prompt:** Begin your prayer by listing three things you're thankful for.
- **Surrender Prompt:** Ask God to take control of specific concerns or decisions.
- **Scripture Prompt:** Meditate on a verse that aligns with

your current challenges or joys.

Tip: Keep a small stack of scripture cards or a devotional book in your prayer space for inspiration. These tools can deepen your reflection, provide guidance for prayer, and prompt meaningful conversations with God.

4. Journal Your Prayers

Documenting your prayers in a journal allows you to track your spiritual journey, reflect on answered prayers, and gain insights into your relationship with God. Writing prayers is especially helpful for those who struggle to stay focused during silent prayer.

Example:

At the end of a challenging day, write a prayer of gratitude and surrender:

Scriptural Anchor:

Proverbs 3:5-6 (NIV):

"Trust in the Lord with all your heart and lean not on your own understanding; in all your ways submit to Him, and He will make your paths straight."

- Start each entry with a verse or reflection.
- Write openly about your struggles, victories, and aspirations.
- Revisit past entries to see how God has worked in your life.

Pro Tip: Use a separate section of your journal to record specific prayer requests and their outcomes, building a tangible reminder of God's faithfulness. Reviewing answered prayers can strengthen your faith, increase gratitude, and provide encouragement during challenging times.

5. Incorporate Silence and Listening

Prayer is not just about speaking to God; it's also about creating space to listen for His guidance. Embrace moments of silence during your prayer time to hear God's voice.

Example:

After praying, spend 2-3 minutes in stillness, meditating on:

Psalm 46:10 (NIV):

"Be still, and know that I am God."

- Practice breath prayer during these moments:
  - **Inhale:** "Speak, Lord,"
  - **Exhale:** "Your servant is listening."

Tip: Silence can be transformative, allowing you to discern God's will and find clarity in your challenges.

6. Pray with Others

Joining others in prayer can strengthen your habit and deepen your sense of community. Group prayers, whether with family, friends, or colleagues, create opportunities for mutual encouragement and shared faith.

Example:

Start or end a team meeting with a short prayer, focusing on wisdom and unity in your work.

Scriptural Inspiration:

Matthew 18:20 (NIV):

"For where two or three gather in my name, there am I with them."

- Host a weekly prayer call or meet-up with fellow Christian professionals.
- Pray with your family at the start or end of each day, cultivating a shared commitment to faith.

The Transformative Power of a Prayer Habit

Developing a prayer habit transforms how you approach challenges, relationships, and decisions. It creates a sacred rhythm in your life, anchoring you in God's presence and aligning your actions with His will.

Final Reflection:

1 Thessalonians 5:17 (NIV):

"Pray continually."

Through prayer, you cultivate resilience, find clarity amidst uncertainty, and deepen your trust in God's plan. By committing to this sacred practice, you can navigate life with peace, purpose, and unwavering faith. Let prayer be the foundation that strengthens your journey, allowing you to stress less and trust God more.

Listening in Prayer: Finding Stillness

Listening in prayer is a profound act of surrender and mindfulness. It allows us to quiet our busy thoughts and tune into God's voice. In a world filled with noise and distractions, this practice offers Christian businesswomen the opportunity to draw closer to God, seek His wisdom, and find strength in His presence. By embracing stillness, you cultivate a deeper connection with God that transforms your spiritual and professional life.

1. Embrace Silence

Silence is the foundation of listening prayer. It creates space for God to speak to your heart, offering guidance and reassurance. Start your prayer time by setting aside distractions—turn off notifications, find a quiet spot, and dedicate this moment solely to God.

Example:

Before starting your workday, spend five minutes in silence, asking God to guide your decisions and actions. Surrender your worries and listen for His reassurance.

Scriptural Anchor:

Isaiah 30:15 (NIV):

“In repentance and rest is your salvation, in quietness and trust is your strength.”

Practical Tips:

- Use noise-canceling headphones or soft instrumental music to block out external distractions.
- Begin with a simple prayer: "Lord, I am here to listen. Speak to my heart."

2. Practice Breath Prayer

Breath prayer is a mindfulness technique that pairs deep breathing with scripture or simple affirmations of faith. This practice helps center your thoughts and calm your spirit, creating an open space to hear God’s voice.

Example Practice:

1. Inhale deeply and silently say: "Jesus."

2. Exhale slowly and say: "I trust in You."

Repeat this for a few minutes, focusing on the rhythm of your breath and the words of the prayer. This rhythmic repetition invites peace into your heart and strengthens your reliance on God.

Scriptural Anchor:

Psalm 46:10 (NIV):

"Be still, and know that I am God."

Benefits:

- Reduces anxiety and stress, creating a calm mindset.
- Reinforces faith in God's guidance and presence.
- Enhances focus and clarity, preparing you for the challenges ahead.

3. Journal Reflections

Writing in a journal after listening to prayer is a valuable method for recording insights, emotions, and revelations. Recording your reflections helps reinforce the lessons God is teaching you and provides a tangible record of your spiritual journey.

Example:

After a session of listening prayer, write about the thoughts or feelings that stood out to you. If a particular scripture resonated, note it, and reflect on its meaning in your life. Consider how God may be speaking to you through that scripture and how it applies to your current circumstances or emotions.

Scriptural Anchor:

Habakkuk 2:2 (NIV):

"Write down the revelation and make it plain on tablets so that a herald may run with it."

Tips for Journaling:

- Use prompts to guide your writing, such as:
  - "What is God teaching me in this moment?"
  - "What am I grateful for today?"
- Review your journal entries regularly to observe patterns, answered prayers, and personal growth. Reflecting on past entries can reveal God's faithfulness, show your progress in spiritual maturity, and provide insights into areas of continued growth and development.

The Transformative Power of Listening in Prayer

Listening prayer is more than a spiritual exercise; it is an invitation to abide in God's presence and trust in His sovereignty. Embracing stillness, engaging in breath prayer, and journaling your reflections help align your heart with God's will and foster a mindset of peace and clarity.

Final Reflection:

Proverbs 3:6 (NIV):

"In all your ways submit to Him, and He will make your paths straight."

As you regularly practice listening to prayer, you will find strength in God's guidance, resilience in challenges, and joy in His unwavering presence. This intentional act of mindfulness and surrender empowers you to navigate life with grace, purpose, and unwavering faith.

The Transformative Power of Prayer as Mindfulness

Prayer is more than a spiritual discipline; it is a transformative practice that integrates faith and mindfulness, enabling Christian businesswomen to navigate their journeys with clarity, strength, and purpose. By engaging in prayer, you create moments of intentionality, allowing space for God's presence to bring peace to your heart and direction to your steps. Prayer becomes a sanctuary for the soul, a wellspring of wisdom, and a cornerstone of resilience in both personal and professional endeavors.

Prayer aligns perfectly with mindfulness principles by encouraging you to focus your heart and mind on the present moment with God, fostering a deeper connection and intentionality. In contrast to secular mindfulness, which often focuses solely on self-awareness, prayer-based mindfulness directs that awareness toward a higher purpose—God's will for your life. Thus, prayer-based mindfulness aligns your intentions with divine guidance.

Example:

Before tackling a challenging task at work, pause to pray: "Lord, grant me clarity and strength as I approach this challenge. Help me to act with integrity and reflect Your love in all I do."

Scriptural Anchor:

Philippians 4:6-7 (NIV):

"Do not be anxious about anything, but in every situation, by prayer and petition, with thanksgiving, present your requests to God. And the peace of God, which transcends all understanding, will guard your hearts and your minds in Christ Jesus."

This practice fosters a spirit of calm and intentionality, reminding you that God is your partner in every endeavor.

Prayer as a Source of Guidance

Prayer offers a direct connection to divine wisdom, guiding you through decisions and challenges. It creates space to discern God's will and ensures that your actions align with His purpose for your life.

Example:

When faced with a critical decision, take a moment to pray for discernment: "Father, illuminate the path You want me to take. Let my choices honor You and serve the greater good."

Scriptural Anchor:

Proverbs 3:5-6 (NIV):

"Trust in the Lord with all your heart and lean not on your own understanding; in all your ways submit to Him, and He will make your paths straight."

By seeking God's guidance through prayer, you can make confident decisions, knowing that His wisdom surpasses all understanding.

Prayer as a Tool for Resilience

Life's challenges may seem overwhelming, but prayer equips you with spiritual strength, empowering you to persevere and overcome adversities. By casting your burdens on God, you free yourself from the weight of anxiety and embrace His peace.

Example:

During moments of stress, practice breath prayer by pairing your breathing with scripture:

- Inhale: "Lord, You are my refuge."

- Exhale: "I trust in Your strength."

Scriptural Anchor:
Isaiah 40:31 (NIV):
"But those who hope in the Lord will renew their strength. They will soar on wings like eagles; they will run and not grow weary; they will walk and not be faint."

Prayer transforms adversity into an opportunity for growth, anchoring you in God's steadfast love and provision.

Final Reflection

Colossians 4:2 (NIV):
"Devote yourselves to prayer, being watchful and thankful."

Through prayer, you invite God into every aspect of your life—your work, relationships, and personal growth. It becomes the cornerstone of mindfulness, helping you remain present, purposeful, and connected to God's will. By integrating prayer into every area of your life, you establish a continuous awareness of God's presence and guidance, fostering a deeper spiritual connection and alignment with His purposes. Developing a prayerful mindset will lead you to a life filled with peace, fulfillment, and steadfast faith.

Let prayer guide your journey, empower your decisions, and renew your spirit daily. By embracing prayer as a mindfulness practice, you transform not only your own life but also the lives of those you inspire, reflecting the light of Christ in all that you do.

CHAPTER 12

MOVING FORWARD WITH PURPOSE

Moving forward with purpose is about living a life of intentionality, where every action, decision, and goal aligns with your core values and faith. For Christian businesswomen, this alignment is not just about achieving success; it is about fulfilling God's unique calling for your life. Purpose gives meaning to your work, fosters resilience during challenges, and inspires others through your example of faith in action. By seeking God's guidance, embracing change with courage, and celebrating growth with gratitude, you can create a life that glorifies God while pursuing your aspirations.

Setting Goals Aligned with Your Values

Setting goals that reflect your core values helps ensure that your beliefs, aspirations, and daily actions are in harmony for long-term success. As a Christian businesswoman, aligning goals with values ensures that your efforts honor God, bring personal fulfillment, and benefit others. Values guide your moral and spiritual beliefs, helping you make decisions and take actions with integrity and purpose.

1. Discover Your Core Values

Understanding your core values is the first step toward meaningful goal-setting. Values are the fundamental beliefs that shape your identity and determine your principles. They act as a filter through which you can evaluate opportunities, challenges, and priorities. When your goals align with your core values, they become more purposeful and fulfilling, ensuring that your actions reflect what truly matters to you. This alignment not only guides your decision-making but also enhances your commitment, as goals rooted in your values resonate with your personal and spiritual convictions.

Reflection and Prayer

Reflecting and praying deepen self-awareness, fostering a connection with God's guidance and helping you discover values that resonate with your soul.

Take intentional time to reflect on what matters most in your life and business. Ask yourself questions such as:

- What brings me the greatest sense of fulfillment?
- What principles do I want to pass on to others?
- How does my faith shape my priorities?

Action Step

Allocate a quiet morning for prayer and journaling. Record the themes that deeply resonate with your heart. Select five core values that define your identity and purpose. For instance, your values could be described as pillars of integrity, stewardship, service, compassion, or excellence in action.

Scriptural Anchor

Proverbs 3:5-6 (NIV):

“Trust in the Lord with all your heart and lean not on your own understanding; in all your ways submit to Him, and He will make your paths straight."

By inviting God into this process, you ensure that your values are grounded in His purpose for your life.

2. Set SMART Goals Aligned with Your Values

Once you've identified your values, the next step is to translate them into actionable goals. Using the SMART framework ensures that your goals are specific, measurable, achievable, relevant, and time-bound.

Examples of Value-Aligned Goals

- **If stewardship is your value:**
  Set a goal to donate 10% of your profits to charitable causes within the next fiscal year.

- **If service is your value:**
  Commit to volunteering three hours a week with a local nonprofit.

- **If excellence is your value:**
  Aim to complete a professional certification within six months to enhance your skills.

Inspiration from Scripture

Matthew 25:21 (NIV):

"Well done, good and faithful servant! You have been faithful with a few things; I will put you in charge of many things. Come and share your master's happiness!"

This verse emphasizes that aligning our goals with God's purpose equips us to embrace greater opportunities with faithfulness and joy.

Practical Example

Break your goals into smaller, actionable milestones to make progress manageable and measurable. For instance, if your goal is to donate a percentage of your business profits to charity, begin by identifying causes that align with your values. Research reputable organizations, set a specific target amount, and create a financial plan to track your giving. Begin with a modest donation, like 1% of profits, and incrementally raise the amount as your business expands. This step-by-step approach ensures that you stay on track while building confidence in your ability to achieve the larger goal.

3. Build Accountability

Accountability is essential for staying on track with your goals. It creates a structure of encouragement and responsibility that keeps you focused and motivated.

Find Supportive Partners

Share your goals with a mentor, prayer partner, or trusted friend. This person can offer encouragement, provide honest feedback, and celebrate your progress.

Example of Accountability

Join a group of like-minded women who meet monthly to discuss goals, share challenges, and pray for one another. This collaborative approach fosters mutual growth and provides a safe space for reflection.

Biblical Insight

Ecclesiastes 4:9-10 (NIV):

"Two are better than one, because they have a good return for their labor: If either of them falls down, one can help the other up. But pity anyone who falls and has no one to help them up."

Involving others in your journey strengthens your determination and fosters a community based on shared faith and purpose.

4. Celebrate Your Values in Action

Celebrating moments when your decisions and actions reflect your values reinforces their importance and inspires continued alignment.

Recognizing progress, no matter how small, fosters gratitude and joy. These emotions not only uplift the spirit but also create a positive feedback loop, enhancing motivation and cultivating a mindset of optimism and resilience, which empowers individuals to continue striving toward their goals with renewed energy and purpose.

Celebrate Milestones

When you achieve a value-driven goal, take time to reflect and thank God for His guidance. Whether it's a successful project, a charitable contribution, or personal growth, each milestone is a testament to your faith and dedication.

Example of Celebration

A businesswoman who values stewardship might celebrate reaching her giving goal by hosting a small dinner to thank her team and share the impact of their contributions.

Scriptural Reflection

Psalm 118:24 (NIV):

"This is the day the Lord has made; let us rejoice and be glad in it."

Celebrating progress is an act of worship that acknowledges God's faithfulness and provision.

5. Evaluate and Adapt

As you move forward, regularly evaluate whether your goals still align with your values and the direction God is leading you. Life's circumstances change, and it's important to adapt with a spirit of flexibility and trust.

Practical Tip

Schedule quarterly check-ins to review your goals. Ask yourself:

- Do these goals still reflect my values?
- How has God been working through these goals?
- What adjustments can I make to stay aligned with His pur-

pose?

Encouragement from Scripture

Isaiah 30:21 (NIV):

"Whether you turn to the right or to the left, your ears will hear a voice behind you, saying, 'This is the way; walk in it.'"

Trust that God will guide you in refining your goals as you seek His direction.

Living Out Your Values Through Your Goals

Setting goals aligned with your values is not just about achieving success; it's about creating a life that glorifies God and reflects His love. Every goal, rooted in faith and purpose, contributes to fulfilling your divine calling.

Final ReflectionColossians 3:23-24 (NIV):

"Whatever you do, work at it with all your heart, as working for the Lord, not for human masters, since you know that you will receive an inheritance from the Lord as a reward."

Let your goals reflect your faith, values, and trust in God's plan for your life. By pursuing them with intentionality and gratitude, you will create a legacy of purpose, impact, and unwavering faith.

Embracing Change and Uncertainty

Change is a constant in life, but for Christian businesswomen, it can be a transformative opportunity to grow spiritually, emotionally, and professionally. When faced with uncertainty, leaning into faith provides strength and assurance, reminding us that God's plan is sovereign and His timing perfect. Embracing change with a mindset of trust and purpose allows you to navigate transitions with grace and courage.

1. Reframe Change as Growth

Though often uncomfortable, change is a powerful catalyst for growth. By reframing challenges as opportunities to evolve, you can approach transitions with hope and resilience. Each change presents a chance to deepen your trust in God and refine your character.

Example: Navigating Career Transitions

When faced with a career shift, whether unexpected or planned, remind yourself of God's faithfulness. Take time to reflect on His promises, like those found in **Jeremiah 29:11 (NIV):** *"For I know the plans I have for you," declares the Lord, "plans to prosper you and not to harm you, plans to give you hope and a future."*

Practical Action Step

During moments of doubt, write down three ways past changes have led to blessings or growth. Reflecting on these experiences reminds you that God is always at work, even in uncertain times.

2. Practice Mindfulness During Uncertainty

Uncertainty can lead to stress and anxiety, but mindfulness offers a way to stay grounded in the present moment. For Christian businesswomen, mindfulness rooted in prayer and scripture can help focus thoughts and find peace amid the unknown.

Mindfulness in Action

Set aside time each day for stillness and reflection. Use prayer and scripture meditation to center your thoughts and calm your spirit. For example, spend five minutes in deep breathing while meditating on **Psalm 46:10 (NIV):** *"Be still, and know that I am God."*

Actionable Tip

When feelings of overwhelm arise, pause and take five deep breaths. With each inhale, silently repeat, "God is with me." With each exhale, say, "I trust in His plan.""

3. Learn from Biblical Examples

The Bible is rich with stories of individuals who faced immense uncertainty yet trusted in God's plan. Reflecting on these examples can inspire confidence and courage during your own seasons of change.

Esther: Courage Amid Uncertainty

Esther's journey from orphan to queen demonstrates the power of trusting God during uncertain times. Her decision to intercede for her people required faith and courage, and her story reminds us that God often positions us for greatness during moments of challenge.

Key Verse:

Esther 4:14 (NIV):

"And who knows but that you have come to your royal position for such a time as this?"

Joseph: Faith Through Trials

Joseph's life—from his brothers' betrayal to his rise to become Egypt's second in command—is a testament to God's redemptive power in the face of adversity. His unwavering faith allowed him to see God's hand even in his darkest moments.

Key Verse:

Genesis 50:20 (NIV):

"You intended to harm me, but God intended it for good to accomplish what is now being done, the saving of many lives."

4. Build a Support Network

Navigating change is easier with a strong support system. Surrounding yourself with people who share your faith and values provides encouragement, wisdom, and perspective.

The Power of Community

Engage with fellow Christian women who understand the challenges of balancing faith, family, and business. Whether through professional groups, Bible studies, or mentorship programs, these connections provide opportunities for shared experiences and mutual growth.

Example:

Join a Christian women's leadership network. Members meet monthly to discuss overcoming challenges, share biblical encouragement, and celebrate victories.

Biblical Inspiration: Ecclesiastes 4:9-10 (NIV): *"Two are better than one, because they have a good return for thlabor. If either of them falls down, one can help the other up. But pity anyone who falls and has no one to help them up."*

5. Trust God's Sovereignty

At the heart of embracing change is the belief that God is in control. Even when circumstances feel uncertain or overwhelming, trust that He is working all things together for your good and His glory.

Faith in God's Timing

God's plan often unfolds in ways we don't expect, but His timing is always perfect. Trusting in His sovereignty allows you to release the need for control and rest in His promises.

Key Verse:

Romans 8:28 (NIV):

"And we know that in all things God works for the good of those who love Him, who have been called according to His purpose."

6. Celebrate Resilience and Growth

Each step you take to embrace change strengthens your resilience and deepens your faith. Celebrate small victories and acknowledge how God is shaping you through these experiences. Gratitude for the journey transforms challenges into blessings.

Practical Celebration Tip

Keep a "Growth Journal" where you document lessons learned, prayers answered, and ways you've grown through seasons of change. Pair each entry with a scripture that resonates with your experience.

Example Entry: *"Today, I saw how God used this career shift to open new doors. Reflecting on Proverbs 16:9 (NIV): 'In their hearts humans plan their course, but the Lord establishes their steps,' I'm reminded that He's guiding me every step of the way."*

Living with Faith-Filled Confidence

Embracing change and uncertainty is a testament to your faith and resilience. By reframing challenges as opportunities for growth, practicing mindfulness, learning from biblical examples, and building a supportive network, you can navigate life's transitions with grace and confidence. Trust that God is with you in every season, guiding your path and strengthening your spirit.

Final Encouragement: Joshua 1:9 (NIV): *"Have I not commanded you? Be strong and courageous. Do not be afraid; do not be discouraged, for the Lord your God will be with you wherever you go."*

Move forward with faith, knowing that God's plans are for your good and His glory.

Celebrating Progress and Growth

Celebrating progress is a practice of gratitude that acknowledges God's faithfulness and nurtures a positive, resilient mindset. It allows Christian businesswomen to pause, reflect, and rejoice in the journey rather than focusing solely on the destination. Recognizing how far you've come enhances your motivation, deepens your faith, and highlights God's role in your growth.

1. Reflect on Achievements

Reflection is a valuable practice for acknowledging how God has guided you through challenges and supported your achievements. Setting aside regular time to evaluate your progress can foster a sense of gratitude and keep you mindful of the journey rather than solely the outcome.

Practical Step: Weekly Reflection

At the end of each week, spend a few moments in quiet reflection. Write down three things you've achieved, no matter how small, and one moment where you felt God's hand guiding you. This practice helps you see progress and divine intervention.

Example: This week, I successfully presented a proposal to a client, learned a new software tool, and organized my workspace. I felt God's presence during the meeting when I prayed for calm and clarity."

Scriptural Anchor:

Psalm 126:3 (NIV):

"The Lord has done great things for us, and we are filled with joy."

2. Celebrate Small Wins

Big accomplishments are built on small, consistent efforts. Celebrating these incremental victories not only reinforces motivation but also shifts your focus from what remains to be done to what has already been achieved.

Example: Celebrate a Challenging Task

After completing a challenging project or reaching a milestone, take a moment to acknowledge your effort. This could be a prayer of thanks, a quiet coffee break, or even writing a short note of gratitude in your journal. Recognize that every step forward is a testament to God's strength working through you.

Inspiration:

Zechariah 4:10 (NLT):

"Do not despise these small beginnings, for the Lord rejoices to see the work begin."

3. Share Your Joy with Others

Celebration is not just a personal experience—it's an opportunity to build community and inspire others. Sharing your successes with loved ones, colleagues, or mentors strengthens relationships and encourages others to celebrate their own progress.

Example: Workplace Celebration

When you or your team reaches a significant milestone, host a small gathering to acknowledge the achievement. Begin with a prayer of gratitude, inviting everyone to reflect on the journey and the lessons learned. This fosters a sense of unity and appreciation.

Biblical Inspiration:

Romans 12:15 (NIV):

"Rejoice with those who rejoice; mourn with those who mourn."

4. Document Your Journey

Creating a tangible record of your progress helps you visualize growth and keeps you motivated. Whether through journaling, a scrapbook, or a vision board, documenting your journey serves as a reminder of God's faithfulness and your resilience.

Example: Gratitude Journal

Dedicate a section of your journal to tracking milestones and answering prayers. Reflect on past entries during moments of doubt or stress to see how God has worked in your life.

Practical Tip:

Use photos, quotes, or scripture verses to complement your records. For instance, add Proverbs 16:3 (NIV):

"Commit to the Lord whatever you do, and He will establish your plans."

5. Praise Through Prayer

Integrate gratitude into your prayer life to celebrate progress. Thank God not only for your accomplishments but also for the strength, guidance, and lessons you have learned along the way.

Example: Prayer of Gratitude

"Lord, thank You for giving me the strength to overcome challenges and the wisdom to make decisions. I am grateful for Your guidance and the opportunities You've placed before me. May I continue to glorify You in all I do."

Scriptural Anchor:

1 Thessalonians 5:18 (NIV):

"Give thanks in all circumstances, for this is God's will for you in Christ Jesus."

6. Foster a Culture of Celebration

Encourage a culture of celebration in your workplace or community by recognizing the efforts and achievements of others. This promotes a positive environment and reinforces the value of collective success.

Example: Team Acknowledgment

At the end of each month, hold a brief team meeting to highlight individual and group accomplishments. Begin with a prayer and end with words of encouragement, creating a space for shared gratitude and motivation.

Biblical Wisdom:

Hebrews 10:24 (NIV):

"And let us consider how we may spur one another on toward love and good deeds."

Living in a Spirit of Gratitude

Celebrating progress and growth means recognizing God's faithfulness at every step of the journey. It shifts the focus from striving for perfection to embracing the process, encouraging a spirit of gratitude and joy.

Final Encouragement:

Philippians 4:4 (NIV):

"Rejoice in the Lord always. I will say it again: Rejoice!"

Celebrate each step forward, no matter how small, as an act of faith and thanksgiving. Through this practice, you cultivate a life filled with purpose, joy, and unwavering trust in God's plan.

Final Reflection

Living with purpose means infusing every aspect of your life—your goals, actions, and mindset—with your core values and unwavering faith. It's about being intentional in your decisions, resilient in the face of challenges, and grateful for every blessing along the journey. Purposeful living is not just a path to personal and professional success but a spiritual practice that honors God and glorifies His name through your work and life.

Scriptural Anchor:

Colossians 3:23-24 (NIV):

"Whatever you do, work at it with all your heart, as working for the Lord, not for human masters, since you know that you will receive an inheritance from the Lord as a reward."

This verse reminds us that every task, whether big or small, is an opportunity to serve God. When you approach life with this perspective, even the most mundane activities are imbued with meaning and significance.

Embrace Change with Courage

Change is inevitable, but it is also an opportunity to grow and trust God more deeply. Embrace uncertainty with the knowledge that His plans are greater than your own. Reflect on Jeremiah 29:11 (NIV):

"For I know the plans I have for you," declares the Lord, "plans to prosper you and not to harm you, plans to give you hope and a future."

Take each new challenge as a chance to learn, adapt, and rely on His guidance. Trust that even in the midst of change, God is shaping you for greater things.

Celebrate Growth with Gratitude

Recognizing your progress nurtures joy and strengthens your faith. Every step forward, no matter how small, is evidence of God's work in your life. Regularly take time to reflect on your achievements and thank Him for His faithfulness.

Psalm 118:24 (NIV):

"This is the day the Lord has made; let us rejoice and be glad in it."

Celebrate the milestones, the lessons learned, and the strength gained. Let gratitude anchor you in the present and propel you toward the future.

Set Goals That Honor Your Values

Purpose-driven goals align your aspirations with God's will and your personal convictions. By setting intentions rooted in your faith and values, you ensure that your journey is both fulfilling and meaningful.

Proverbs 16:3 (NIV):

"Commit to the Lord whatever you do, and He will establish your plans."

Take time to prayerfully consider your goals and seek accountability from trusted mentors or friends. Let your values guide you toward endeavors that glorify God and contribute to His kingdom.

Moving Forward with Confidence

As you step into the next chapter of your life, carry with you the assurance that God walks beside you. His presence brings peace, His Word offers wisdom, and His promises give hope. Live purposefully, stay strong in your faith, and believe that God has abundant and purposeful plans for you.

Final Encouragement:

Philippians 4:13 (NIV):

"I can do all this through Him who gives me strength."

Let this truth empower you to move forward with boldness and confidence, knowing that the Creator Himself equips, calls, and guides you. Step into your purpose with faith, gratitude, and determination to impact the world for His glory.

CHAPTER 13

RESOURCES AND TOOLS FOR CONTINUED GROWTH

Navigating the complexities of business while nurturing your faith is both a calling and a challenge that requires intentional effort, practical tools, and reliable resources. As Christian businesswomen, balancing professional ambitions with spiritual growth is not only possible but deeply rewarding. By incorporating the right books, podcasts, mindfulness apps, and personal practices into your routine, you can cultivate resilience, clarity, and a deeper connection to God.

This chapter is designed to empower you with actionable tools to support your journey toward mindfulness, stress management, and purposeful living. Whether you're looking for guidance on building a daily routine, strengthening your leadership skills, or aligning your work with your faith, these resources will provide inspiration and practical strategies to help you thrive in every aspect of your life.

Here's what you'll discover in this chapter:

- **Recommended Books and Podcasts**: A curated selection of books and podcasts that blend spiritual wisdom with practical advice, helping you navigate the intersection of faith and business. From inspirational memoirs to actionable guides, these resources are tailored to support your growth as a Christian leader.

- **Mindfulness Apps and Tools**: Explore digital platforms that integrate mindfulness practices with faith-based content, offering guided meditations, daily devotionals, and techniques to stay grounded amidst the demands of business life.

- **Building a Personal Library**: Learn how to create a library of faith and mindfulness resources tailored to your journey, complete with tips on selecting impactful reads and organizing a dedicated space for reflection and growth.

- **Practical Application**: Discover actionable steps to integrate these tools into your daily life, ensuring that your faith remains at the center of your decisions and goals.

As you explore these resources, you'll find encouragement to pursue professional excellence while staying anchored in your spiritual values. These tools are more than just aids for growth; they are companions in your journey, equipping you to face challenges with confidence and embrace opportunities with a sense of divine purpose.

"Let the wise listen and add to their learning, and let the discerning get guidance." – Proverbs 1:5 (NIV)

Let this chapter be your guide to equipping yourself with the knowledge, skills, and spiritual nourishment needed to grow as a mindful, faith-driven businesswoman. Whether you're at the beginning of your journey or looking to deepen your practices, these resources will inspire and empower you to move forward with purpose.

Recommended Books and Podcasts

Books and podcasts serve as valuable sources of wisdom, providing both practical guidance and spiritual inspiration. These resources help Christian businesswomen navigate challenges while staying grounded in faith.

1. **Books to Inspire and Empower**

    - **"Fit for His Purpose: A Christian Woman's Guide to Health & Wellness" by Love Christophers** provides insights on how to prioritize physical health alongside spiritual well-being.

This book is an inspiring and empowering guide that seamlessly blends faith and wellness, offering Christian women practical tools to honor their bodies as temples of the Holy Spirit (1 Corinthians 6:19-20). It addresses physical, emotional, and spiritual health, providing actionable steps to cultivate balance, resilience, and purpose in every aspect of life.

1. ***"Resilient in Christ: Exploring the Intersection of Faith and Mental Health" by Love Christophers*** *offers a unique perspective on maintaining holistic well-being through a strong foundation in faith.*

This book is an empowering guide that blends faith and mental health. It offers Christian women tools to manage anxiety, overcome burnout, and build resilience. Through scripture and practical strategies, it inspires readers to embrace healing, break the stigma surrounding mental health, and rely on God's strength for renewal. Perfect for those seeking peace and purpose, this book provides hope and guidance for thriving in every season.

1. ***"The Gift of Grace: Unlocking the Power of Favor" by Love Christophers*** *is a must-read for anyone looking to transform their lives and find joy in the midst of struggles.*

This book is an inspiring exploration of God's unmerited favor, offering Christian women a deeper understanding of grace in their daily lives. This book illuminates how embracing God's grace can transform challenges into opportunities, renew your spirit, and empower you to live a life of abundance and purpose. Through relatable stories, scriptural insights, and practical applications, it serves as a guide to unlocking the power of favor in your spiritual journey. Perfect for those seeking encouragement, this book reveals how God's grace equips us to thrive and shine in every season of life.

1. ***"Leading with Grace: A Christian Woman's Approach to Purpose-Driven Leadership" by Love Christophers*** *empowers women to step into their calling with confidence and strength.*

This book offers a transformative guide for Christian women seeking to lead with intention, wisdom, and faith. This empowering book delves into the essence of purpose-driven leadership, providing practical strategies grounded in scripture. It explores how to balance professional demands with spiritual integrity, foster meaningful relationships, and navigate challenges with grace and resilience. Perfect for women in leadership roles or aspiring to make a greater impact, this book inspires readers to embrace their God-given calling and lead with authenticity, compassion, and purpose. Whether in the workplace, community, or home, this is an essential resource for women who strive to lead for His glory.

1. ***"Love Anchored: A Christian Woman's Guide to Dating with Purpose" by Love Christophers***

This book is an inspiring and practical resource for Christian women seeking to approach dating with faith and intentionality. It offers biblical wisdom, personal stories, and actionable advice on navigating relationships, setting boundaries, and discerning God's will. Designed to empower women to remain grounded in their values, this guide encourages patience, confidence, and trust in God's plan for finding meaningful, lasting love.

1. **"The Mindful Christian: Cultivating a Life of Intentionality, Openness, and Faith" by Shona Murray**
   This book bridges mindfulness with Christian teachings, providing actionable strategies to remain present in both personal and professional settings.
   Takeaway: Learn how to integrate faith into your daily routine through mindfulness practices grounded in scripture.

2. **"Present Over Perfect: Leaving Behind Frantic for a Simpler, More Soulful Way of Living" by Shauna Niequist**
   Niequist's personal journey inspires women to prioritize meaningful living over perfection, emphasizing simplicity and soul care.
   Key Verse: Matthew 6:33 (NIV): "But seek first His kingdom and His righteousness, and all these things will be given to you as well."

3. **"Sacred Rhythms: Arranging Our Lives for Spiritual Transformation" by Ruth Haley Barton**
   This book explores spiritual disciplines that foster a deeper

relationship with God, making it an excellent resource for mindful living.

4. **Podcasts for Growth and Encouragement**

    - **"The Mindful Christian Podcast"**
      Featuring discussions on mindfulness from a biblical perspective, this podcast is ideal for busy professionals seeking practical insights.

    - **"The Happy Mind Podcast"**
      Combining mindfulness and productivity, this podcast offers strategies to cultivate joy and reduce stress in work and life.

    - **"She Works His Way"**
      Tailored for Christian women in business, this podcast addresses the challenges of balancing career, faith, and family.

Action Step: Dedicate time each week to reading one book or podcast and reflecting on how its lessons can be applied to your life and career.

Mindfulness Apps and Tools

Mindfulness apps are excellent for integrating moments of stillness and reflection into a busy schedule. For Christian businesswomen, apps with spiritual content can enhance both mindfulness and faith.

1. **Top Apps for Mindfulness and Faith**

    - **Abide**
      A Christian meditation app offering guided prayers, scripture readings, and mindfulness exercises designed to

deepen your spiritual connection.

- **Calm**
  Known for its soothing meditations, breathing exercises, and sleep aids, Calm also allows for personal reflection through its customizable tools.

- **Bible App by YouVersion**
  This app includes daily devotionals, Bible reading plans, and inspirational reminders that can be seamlessly incorporated into mindfulness routines.

2. **Features to Look For**

   - **Guided Meditations**
     Sessions that combine scripture and mindfulness, helping you remain present while focusing on God's word.

   - **Journaling Prompts**
     Tools that encourage reflection and gratitude.

   - **Community Features**
     Some apps connect you with like-minded individuals for mutual encouragement.

Example: Use Abide's guided scripture meditation during a morning break to center yourself before a busy workday. Pair this with Psalm 46:10 (NIV): "Be still, and know that I am God."

Building a Personal Library of Faith and Mindfulness

Curating a personal library dedicated to faith and mindfulness is a transformative practice for Christian businesswomen. It is more than just a collection of books; it is a sanctuary of wisdom, a resource for navigating challenges, and a constant reminder of your spiritual and professional aspirations. A thoughtfully curated library becomes a place where you can draw inspiration, find solace, and deepen your connection with God.

1. **Selecting Your Materials**

When building your library, focus on materials that resonate with your values and aspirations. Choose a mix of classic, contemporary, and practical works to support your journey.

1. **Classics on Faith**

    - Include timeless works that have shaped Christian thought. Books like *The Imitation of Christ* by Thomas à Kempis or *Mere Christianity* by C.S. Lewis offer profound insights into living a life rooted in faith.
    - These classics can serve as anchors, providing a foundation of spiritual wisdom that transcends generations.

2. **Modern Perspectives**

    - Contemporary authors bring fresh perspectives to timeless principles.
    - Consider *One Thousand Gifts* by Ann Voskamp, which explores the transformative power of gratitude, or *Boundaries* by Dr. Henry Cloud, which provides actionable guidance on maintaining healthy relationships and work-life balance.
    - These books offer relatable insights that address the complexities of modern Christian living.

3. **Mindfulness and Spiritual Growth**

- Expand your library to include books that integrate mindfulness with faith.
- *The Miracle of Mindfulness* by Thich Nhat Hanh focuses on cultivating presence and intentionality, which can complement your spiritual practices.
- Look for resources that align with biblical teachings while helping you remain present in your daily walk with God.

4. **Creating a Sacred Reading Space**

Transform a corner of your home or office into a dedicated space for reading and reflection.

1. **Comfortable and Inviting**: To make the space inviting, choose a cozy chair, good lighting, and soothing elements like soft blankets or cushions.
2. **Meaningful Decor**: Add personal touches that inspire you, such as a Bible, a prayer journal, candles, or framed scripture verses. These items create a sacred atmosphere and help focus your mind.
3. **Scriptural Anchors**: Display your favorite verses, like Jeremiah 29:11 (NIV):
   "For I know the plans I have for you," declares the Lord, "plans to prosper you and not to harm you, plans to give you hope and a future."
   Such reminders reinforce your spiritual goals and provide encouragement during challenging moments.
4. **Active Engagement with Texts**

While reading passively is helpful, engaging actively with your materials can deepen your understanding and create a lasting impact.

1. **Highlight and Reflect**
    - Highlight key passages that resonate with you and jot down your reflections in the margins or a dedicated notebook.
    - Write down how specific lessons apply to your life or business decisions, making the readings personal and actionable.
2. **Journaling**
    - Use a journal to document how the teachings influence your spiritual growth and professional journey.
    - Reflect on how these insights align with your goals and values.
3. **Share and Discuss**
    - Share impactful insights with a small group, prayer circle, or colleagues who adhere to your faith.
    - Engage in discussions that challenge and deepen your understanding, fostering community and mutual growth.

Example: Vision Board of Inspiration

In your sacred reading space, create a vision board with quotes, scriptures, and personal goals. Include passages like Proverbs 3:5-6 (NIV):

"Trust in the Lord with all your heart and lean not on your own understanding; in all your ways submit to Him, and He will make your paths straight."

Use the vision board to visually connect your readings with your aspirations, reinforcing your commitment to living a purposeful, faith-driven life.

Final Reflection

Your personal library of faith and mindfulness is more than a collection of books—it is a testament to your commitment to growth, faith, and purpose. Let this sanctuary inspire you to live intentionally, align your actions with God's will, and navigate the complexities of life with grace and wisdom.

"Let the word of Christ dwell in you richly, teaching and admonishing one another in all wisdom." – Colossians 3:16 (ESV)

Engaging with a Supportive Community

Building and participating in a supportive community is essential for Christian businesswomen seeking to grow spiritually and professionally. By surrounding yourself with like-minded individuals, you create a network that fosters accountability, encouragement, and shared wisdom. This sense of belonging amplifies the impact of the resources and tools you utilize while inspiring collective growth.

1. **Join Faith-Based Groups**

   a. **Christian Women's Business Networks**

      - Connect with groups that share your values and professional aspirations. These communities provide opportunities for mentorship, collaboration, and mutual support.

      - For example, you could join organizations like

Christian Women in Business or local church-based business forums to connect with women who are navigating similar challenges and triumphs.

b. **Bible Study Groups for Professionals**

- Participate in Bible studies designed for working women. These groups often explore topics like leadership, integrity, and stewardship from a biblical perspective.
- Example: Create or join a lunchtime Bible study group at your workplace where participants can discuss how to apply scripture to business decisions.

c. **Online Faith-Based Communities**

- Engage with social media groups, forums, or virtual communities that focus on faith and entrepreneurship. These platforms allow you to connect with others globally, sharing experiences and resources.
- Example: Join a Facebook group or LinkedIn community for Christian entrepreneurs to exchange advice, celebrate wins, and seek prayers during challenges.

2. **Collaborative Learning**

a. **Organize Book Clubs or Study Sessions**

- Gather colleagues or friends to discuss books, articles, or devotionals that focus on spiritual and professional growth.

- Example: Start a monthly book discussion focusing on works like *Present Over Perfect* by Shauna Niequist or *Boundaries* by Dr. Henry Cloud. Open each session with prayer and conclude by brainstorming ways to apply the lessons.

b. **Workshops, Retreats, and Conferences**

- Attend events designed for Christian businesswomen to learn from experts, share experiences, and deepen your faith. These gatherings often feature inspirational speakers, networking opportunities, and practical workshops.

- Example: Attend a Christian leadership conference that combines professional development with spiritual renewal. Bring back actionable insights to implement in your business or workplace.

c. **Peer Accountability Groups**

- Form small groups where members set goals, track progress, and provide encouragement. These groups can meet weekly or monthly to ensure consistent growth.

- Example: Establish a "Faith and Goals" group where members pray for each other's endeavors, celebrate milestones, and discuss strategies to overcome obstacles.

Example of a Monthly Book Discussion

- **Theme**: Faith and Professional Growth
- **Structure**:
  - **Opening Prayer**: Set the tone by inviting God's presence into the discussion.
  - **Discussion**: Share insights, favorite quotes, or key takeaways from the selected book.
  - **Practical Application**: Brainstorm how to apply the lessons learned in daily life and business.
  - **Closing Reflection**: End with gratitude and a prayer for wisdom and guidance.

Scriptural Inspiration for Community

Hebrews 10:24-25 (NIV):

"And let us consider how we may spur one another on toward love and good deeds, not giving up meeting together, as some are in the habit of doing, but encouraging one another—and all the more as you see the Day approaching."

Engaging with a supportive community is a biblical practice that strengthens faith and empowers one to confidently pursue one's calling.

Final Thought

By intentionally connecting with a network of faith-driven women, you cultivate an environment where shared learning and mutual encouragement thrive. This community not only supports you in achieving your goals but also reinforces the values and faith that guide your journey. Together, you grow stronger, wiser, and more resilient, bringing glory to God in all you do.

Final Reflection

Equipping yourself with resources and tools for continued growth is not merely about enhancing your skills or achieving success—it is about aligning every step of your journey with God's divine purpose. Growth is both a personal and spiritual pursuit, and as Christian businesswomen, this alignment ensures that your actions glorify God while positively impacting those around you.

Colossians 3:17 (NIV) serves as a poignant reminder of this truth:

"And whatever you do, whether in word or deed, do it all in the name of the Lord Jesus, giving thanks to God the Father through him."

This verse challenges us to integrate faith into every aspect of our lives—our words, deeds, and ambitions—making them acts of worship and gratitude.

By intentionally leveraging books, podcasts, apps, and communities, you can navigate life's complexities with clarity, resilience, and purpose. These resources not only enhance your ability to manage stress, build mindfulness, and foster personal growth but also keep you anchored in God's promises.

Let **intentionality** guide your decisions, ensuring your goals reflect your core values. Let **tenacity** propel you forward, giving you the strength to overcome challenges with courage and grace. Most importantly, let a **dedication to exalting God** in all that you do remain at the heart of your journey.

As you move forward, remember that your growth is not solely for your benefit but also for God's glory. Each step, whether big or small, is part of a greater plan—His plan for you to thrive, inspire, and fulfill your calling. Trust in His guidance, lean on His strength, and celebrate the abundant opportunities to reflect His light in your work and life.

REFERENCES

1. American Heart Association. (2019). "The Impact of Stress on Heart Health."

2. American Psychological Association. (2022). "Stress in America."

3. American Psychological Association. (2022). "Stress and Its Impact on Health."

4. Boubekri, M., Cheung, I. N., Reid, K. J., Wang, C. H., & Zee, P. C. (2014). *Impact of windows and daylight exposure on overall health and sleep quality.* Journal of Clinical Sleep Medicine, 10(6), 603-611.

5. Brown, R. P., & Gerbarg, P. L. (2005). Sudarshan Kriya yogic breathing in the treatment of stress, anxiety, and depression: Part I—neurophysiologic model. *Journal of Alternative and Complementary Medicine*, 11(1), 189-201.

6. Clance, P. R., & Imes, S. A. (1978). "The Imposter Phenomenon." *Psychotherapy Theory, Research, and Practice.*

7. Cohen, S., Janicki-Deverts, D., & Miller, G. E. (2007). "Psychological Stress and Disease." *JAMA.*

8. Cohen, S., & Wills, T. A. (1985). Stress, social support, and the buffering hypothesis. *Psychological Bulletin*, 98(2), 310–357.

9. Emmons, R. A., & McCullough, M. E. (2003). Counting blessings versus burdens: An experimental investigation of gratitude and subjective well-being. *Journal of Personality and Social Psychology*.

10. Foster, R. J. (1998). *Celebration of Discipline: The Path to Spiritual Growth.*

11. Journal of Psychology and Christianity. "Christian Mindfulness: A Pathway to Spiritual and Emotional Growth" (2014).

12. Kabat-Zinn, J. (2013). *Full Catastrophe Living: Using the Wisdom of Your Body and Mind to Face Stress, Pain, and Illness.*

13. Keating, T. (2008). *Intimacy with God: An Introduction to Centering Prayer.*

14. Krause, N., & Hayward, R. D. (2013). Religious involvement, practical wisdom, and well-being. *Journal of Psychology and Christianity*.

15. Laird, M. (2006). *Into the Silent Land: A Guide to the Christian Practice of Contemplation.*

16. LeanIn.org. (2022). *Women in the Workplace 2022.*

17. Mayer, E. (2011). *The Mind-Gut Connection.*

18. McGinn, B. (1991). *The Foundations of Mysticism: Origins to the Fifth Century.*

19. McKinsey & Company. (2022). "Women in the Workplace."

20. National Sleep Foundation. (2020). "Sleep and Stress."

21. Pennebaker, J. W. (1997). Writing about emotional experiences as a therapeutic process. *Psychological Science.*

22. Pew Research Center. (2021). "Gender Differences in Work-Life Balance."

23. Sandi, C. (2013). "Stress and Cognitive Function." *Nature Reviews Neuroscience.*

24. Sapolsky, R. M. (2004). *Why Zebras Don't Get Ulcers.*

25. Seligman, M. E. P., Steen, T. A., Park, N., & Peterson, C. (2005). Positive Psychology Progress: Empirical Validation of Interventions. *American Psychologist, 60*(5), 410–421.

26. Sinha, R., & Jastreboff, A. M. (2011). Stress as a common risk factor for obesity and addiction. *Biological Psychiatry,* 73(9), 827-835.

27. Smyth, J. M., & Pennebaker, J. W. (2018). Exploring the health benefits of expressive writing. *Psychological Science in the Public Interest.*

28. Vohs, K. D., Redden, J. P., & Rahinel, R. (2013). *Physical order produces healthy choices, generosity, and conventionality, whereas disorder produces creativity.* Psychological Science, 24(9), 1860-1867.

29. Weil, A. (2011). *Breathing: The Master Key to Self-Healing.*

30. Wood, A. M., Froh, J. J., & Geraghty, A. W. A. (2010). Gratitude and Well-Being: A Review and Theoretical Integration. *Clinical Psychology Review, 30*(7), 890–905.

31. Zimmerman, B. J., & Schunk, D. H. (2011). *Self-regulated learning and academic achievement: Theoretical perspectives.* Springer.

New International Version (NIV). Holy Bible. Biblica, 1973, 1978, 1984, 2011.

New International Version (NIV). Holy Bible. Biblica, 2011. Accessed from Bible Gateway

King James Version (KJV). Holy Bible. Originally published in 1611, public domain.

King James Version (KJV). Holy Bible. 1611. Accessed from Bible Gateway

English Standard Version (ESV). Holy Bible. Copyright © 2001, Crossway, a publishing ministry of Good News Publishers. All rights reserved.

English Standard Version (ESV). Holy Bible. 2001. Accessed from ESV.org

www.ingramcontent.com/pod-product-compliance
Lightning Source LLC
La Vergne TN
LVHW041207150826
845673LV00001B/311